ANYTHING
BUT
BLAND

Moxie, Murdaugh, and Making Life Happen on Your Own Terms

ERIC BLAND

This book is memoir. It reflects the author's present recollections of experiences over time. Some names, dates, locations and characteristics have been changed, some events have been compressed, and some dialogue has been recreated. This book represents the personal views and opinions of the author and does not necessarily reflect the positions or opinions of any organization, institution, or individual with which the author is affiliated. The content presented herein is based on the author's perspective and interpretation of the subject matter. Neither the publisher, distributor, nor any associated parties shall be held responsible for any consequences arising from the opinions or interpretations expressed within this book.

Editing, design, distribution by Bublish
Cover photo © Kayla Balderson

ISBN: 978-1-64704-867-9 (Paperback)
ISBN: 978-1-64704-868-6 (Hardcover)
ISBN: 978-1-64704-866-2 (eBook)
ISBN: 978-1-64704-870-9 (Audiobook)

DEDICATION

This book is dedicated to my parents Howard and Mollie Bland, as well as my amazing wife, Renée, and our two children, Dr. Sydney Bland and Davis Bland. They have all sacrificed so much for me to achieve my dreams.

I am also grateful for the sacrifices made by Renee's parents, Bob and Edna Culp, who personally guaranteed and obtained a loan for me to open my law practice when I moved with Renee from Philadelphia to South Carolina in 1991. Not a day goes by where I do not take a moment to recognize the profound impact of your belief in me.

Also, to my law partner and brother-in-arms, Ronnie Richter Jr. Striving for greatness with you has been the honor of my life. What an amazing ride we've had together so far!

Love,
EB

TABLE OF CONTENTS

CHAPTER 1

SWEAT MORE NOW, BLEED LESS LATER

"Suffer now and live the rest of your life as a champion."

—*Muhammad Ali*

"**H**e's a despicable, evil person, but he's a damn good criminal."
It was June 4, 2022, and I was sitting with my law partner,
Ronnie Richter, being interviewed by Will Folks, founding editor of FITSNews in South Carolina. That's when we made our
predictions about the infamous South Carolina attorney Alex
Murdaugh.

"Yes, I think he's a damn good criminal, but he's not that
smart," Ronnie chimed in after my comment. "Who will probably never see daylight again."

"He shouldn't, and he won't." I agreed.

We all knew a bombshell was about to drop in the
Murdaugh investigation but couldn't talk about it publicly yet.
In that moment, though, we were confident Alex Murdaugh
was finally going to be brought to justice after using his wealth,

influence, and power to terrorize the people of Hampton County, South Carolina, for decades.

That same week, I'd been interviewed by CNN, CBS, ABC, and NPR. As the legal team representing some of the families from whom Murdaugh had stolen millions, Ronnie and I were doing a lot of television, newspaper, and podcast interviews, as well as documentaries for Netflix, Disney, and Fox. But somewhere along the way, I had become the public face of the state's case against Murdaugh, mostly due to my close working relationship with Assistant Attorney General Creighton Waters. Why me? Well, I understood the power of the press and had a good relationship with them. I knew the legal details of the case like the back of my hand. And I had a mouth on me. It had gotten me in a lot of trouble as a kid but would prove to be an invaluable asset as a lawyer. Most importantly, I believed in the prosecution and the evidence against Alex Murdaugh. At the time, I was one of the few attorneys willing to publicly criticize Murdaugh's defense team.

My involvement with the Murdaugh trial began on September 10, 2021, a day that began like most any other in my then thirty-three-year law career. I went to the gym, got to work before 8:00 a.m., and decided which client and legal matter would be the object of my attention that morning. I had never met Alex Murdaugh, or known much about him, other than what I'd read in the papers or heard in the news. There was the strange Mallory Beach boating accident, the murders of Murdaugh's wife, Maggie, and son Paul, and the bizarre Labor Day shooting incident by the side of the road near the Murdaugh family's hunting estate in Moselle, South Carolina. Alex Murdaugh's law firm—Peters, Murdaugh, Parker, Eltzroth & Detrick (PMPED)—had a unique mystique in our legal community. The firm was prestigious and commanding, but no one was sure what the lawyers there did, other than make piles of money. No one outside of Hampton County had a clue about what was really going on inside the secretive Murdaugh dynasty—but we would all soon find out, and the revelations would be horrifying.

For most of my legal career, my work with Ronnie has involved suing other lawyers and professionals. It's what our firm—Bland Richter, in Columbia, South Carolina—does. We handle legal and medical malpractice cases and highly contested business disputes. We take down professionals who don't do right by their clients or patients. It is a tough and often toxic job. Our work is not popular. We are universally disliked by judges and lawyers across the state. Yet, ironically, many of them refer us to cases—as long as we don't share their names. They get tired of watching the legal corruption and malfeasance, so they turn on their colleagues. What's the saying? "Friends come and go but enemies accumulate." We see a lot of that in our business.

I guess that's why I shouldn't have been surprised by what happened on the morning of September 10, 2021—but I was. The phone rang. It was Mark Tinsley, an excellent trial attorney from Allendale, South Carolina, whom I'd known for years. When I first met Mark, we were adversaries on different sides of a fee dispute case. I believed Mark hated me because I'd brought a lawsuit against him. But after the case ended, we discovered that we practiced law and lived life similarly and developed a surprising friendship. He would often refer potential legal matters to me. Our conversation that morning began like any other.

"Eric, how are you?"

"Good, Mark. Long time. What's up?"

"You want to get knee-deep in the Murdaugh mess?"

I didn't pause. "Sure. Why not? Give it to me."

"Are you sitting down?"

"Uh, yes, I am now. Go ahead. Give it to me straight."

"You know those statements from Murdaugh's firm about all the missing money? Well, it turns out he was actually ripping off his clients."

"What?!" I immediately asked Ronnie to join the call.

"Yeah, Eric, big-time. And you know this isn't what I do. I don't sue lawyers. But you do. So, do you want in?"

Again, I didn't hesitate. "Yes, Ronnie and I want in. Definitely count us in."

Mark began describing a potential case where Alex Murdaugh had allegedly stolen the entire settlement amount from his clients, who were the sons of Murdaugh's former house-keeper, who had died after a fall at one of Murdaugh's homes. Ronnie and I were both astonished and skeptical. Neither of us had ever heard of a case where a lawyer had stolen an entire settlement! The allegations Mark had shared were *really* bad. Was Murdaugh really capable of some of the things we were hearing? It was hard to believe, but we wanted a seat at the table. Both of us knew it would be a historic case because of the Murdaugh family's long-standing prominence in South Carolina. Ironically, just a few months earlier, as suspicions of wrongdoing against Murdaugh had started to mount, I'd told Ronnie that somehow, we would become involved.

After hanging up the phone, Ronnie and I began discussing Mark's call.

"Damn, Eric, you were right!" Ronnie said.

And that's how our collision course with Alex Murdaugh kicked off.

Or was it?

If I'm being honest, my whole career—hell, my whole life—had prepared me for this moment. It felt like destiny. I'd been training thirty-three years for this epic battle with one of the most powerful and corrupt men in South Carolina. I just didn't realize it until Mark called me. Conversely, I'm sure Alex Murdaugh never thought two mutts like Ronnie and me would sink our teeth into his hide and chase him to the gates of hell in order to get redress for some of the people he'd harmed. Murdaugh was preying on the weak and vulnerable— and Ronnie and I were going to help put an end to it. Helping victims was the reason I'd gone into law in the first place. It's still what gets me out of bed in the morning and keeps me up at night. I get angry whenever I hear a story about a lawyer betraying their client.

That's how life works, right? You never know when you'll get your shot—a moment that calls upon all your unique talents, all the skills you've honed over the years, all your experience, all your courage, and the very principles by which you live. I believe everyone gets at least one chance in life to stand up and take on something momentous. The Murdaugh saga was my moment. Everything was on the line, and all the challenges and sacrifices I'd made along the way finally made sense. How Ronnie and I responded to this moment would show the world what Bland Richter was truly made of. We'd either bring it or miss our shot.

On September 10, 2021, I was ready, and so was Ronnie. The Navy SEALs have a motto: "The more you sweat in training, the less you bleed in battle." I'd been sweating it out in training for decades, and I was going to make Murdaugh bleed in front of all his victims—and there were many. These victims deserved justice, and we were going to help them get it.

This is why I do what I do. It's who I am.

But I wasn't always this way. In fact, as a kid, I was a troublemaker with a loose mouth. I let adversity wreak havoc on my life and shape my thoughts and behaviors. I wasn't willing to do the hard work to make myself and my life better. I let circumstances and so-called friends dictate my choices, which led me to make a lot of stupid mistakes. I was a follower, not a leader. But looking back, it all makes sense now. It was the journey I had to take to become the person I am today—and, of course, like all of us, I'm still a work in progress. Fortunately, these days I lead more than follow.

I wrote *Anything But Bland* to share my personal and professional journey with all those who feel stuck or scared, for those who think they can't catch a break or reach their potential.

I know those feelings all too well. I still battle them every day—but now I don't succumb. Negative feelings, experiences, and behaviors can't hold you back if you don't let them. We can try to deny it, but most of us have our demons—and sometimes they can be suffocating. Like everything else, how we deal with our baggage is a choice. I was a punk, but life had a few big surprises in store for me. Luckily, none of them killed me or landed me in jail—even though many of them should have. But they all shaped me into the man I am today—still imperfect, but so much stronger. How I ended up becoming a key member of the legal team that took down one of the most notorious criminals of modern times is a tale of second chances. We all get them, but it's what we do with them that makes all the difference.

CHAPTER 2

FANS ARE BETTER THAN FEARS

"You miss 100 percent of the shots you don't take."

—Wayne Gretzky

T he strong, confident man who went head-to-head with the notorious Alex Murdaugh in the courtroom, and who talked to news organizations around the world as the case evolved, is not the same as the little boy that still lives inside that man and reminds him of his humble roots and troubled past every day. I am a study in contrasts, a complex man who finally discovered and embraced his calling—the pursuit of justice. My journey has been anything but a straight path, and several times, I almost fell—or jumped—off a cliff.

I grew up in a very tight-knit Jewish family. My grandparents emigrated from Kiev, Russia, and Odessa in the Ukraine, to escape the pogroms there in the early 1900s. It was a very difficult crossing, and my maternal grandfather lost two sisters on the boat ride to Ellis Island. But America was an emerging beacon of hope in a dark world, and many risked everything to get here, including my family.

When my father was born in Philadelphia, his last name was Bladstein. As a first-generation American, he graduated from Penn State University with a plan to go to law school or medical school. But at the time, there were quotas for the number of Jews that could be accepted. Remember, this was only a decade after the Holocaust. To circumvent these quotas, my grandfather Albert legally changed his surname to Bland, which was culturally neutral and would shield the family from World War II's lingering antisemitism. As a dentist, my grandfather also believed the name change would ensure his dental practice could attract more than just Jewish patients.

From a young age, I knew being Jewish meant being different. I distinctly remember driving with my grandfather Albert. When police were in the vicinity, his shoulders would go up and his back would straighten.

"Eric! Shhh! Shhh! The shamus, the shamus," he would say, which means the police in Yiddish.

Inadvertently, my grandparents were training us to be ever watchful, ever on high alert. As second-generation Americans, my two brothers and I didn't fully understand why, but our grandparents, parents, and our DNA seemed to tell us that being Jewish meant we must live with fear and always be cautious and cognizant of our surroundings.

As one of the smaller kids in school, I certainly lived with fear when I was young. I was skinny and had no muscles. I was bullied almost every day. Each day I went off to school, I was full of utter and complete dread. I'll never forget what it felt like to go home after a long day of being bullied. The sheer exhaustion and relief you feel when you arrive home safely after school is hard to describe. But those who have been bullied know that exhaustion all too well. You're also scared about going to school the next day because you don't want it to happen again, and these fears make you feel inadequate. *God, I can't even stand up for myself,* is the kind of negative messaging that relentlessly loops through your brain. You're disgusted with yourself, and you don't want to tell your parents or siblings because you don't want them to fight your battles. All day long, you have a pit in your stomach. You're always looking over your shoulder, afraid to go to the bathroom or the locker room in the gym.

The feelings get most intense at night. My mind used to race as I tried to figure out how I would survive the next day. I couldn't go to the principal because I'd be mocked and the bullying would get worse. But I also knew if I tried to fight the bullies, I'd get my ass beaten. You can't reason with bullies, so I'd lie there on my bed, plotting out how to stick with my biggest friends between classes so they could protect me. After I'd crafted my daily survival plan, I'd fall asleep, but then Jimmy Colson's menacing face would turn my dreams into nightmares. He was a classic bully who came from a rough family. He wasn't the brightest student, but he was big and tough. He would call me "Jew Boy" in front of the class. One time, he threw pennies under my desk and made me pick them all up. Everyone laughed. I hated myself for not fighting back. I could see him watching me in the halls and as I walked into the bathroom, where he'd often come after me. I'd start shaking like a coward, which made me feel even worse.

I would ultimately survive the bullies, but battling fear and insecurity would become a constant in my life. As an adult, I would realize that if I didn't harness these powerful emotions, they would harness me—and I refused to let that happen.

* * *

When my father finished his undergraduate years, our new family surname came in handy. Howard Bland did get into law school, which made my grandfather Albert very proud. But my dad didn't like it. He left after only a year and ended up working for the remainder of his career as a traveling salesman. He sold polyethylene film—which is shrunk around boats and cars as a layer of protection as well as used in agriculture. My father's job meant he was on the road a lot. Over the years, he worked for several of the largest companies in the industry, like Diamond Shamrock and Plicose. He didn't make a lot of money, so vacations were rare, but sometimes, he took me with him on business trips. I think it was a way to get me away from the bullies.

When I was twelve, we were passing through Maryland, which was part of his territory, and my dad decided to take me to the ACC basketball finals. It was 1974, and Maryland was playing North Carolina State. Our family's whole lives revolved around basketball. We were all big fans and played throughout our childhoods. My two brothers, Robbie and Richie, who were older and much taller and stronger than me, played on different teams. My dad coached us all and never missed our games. At that time, the ACC had some of the best basketball players—David Thompson, Monte Towe, Tom Burleson, Bobby Jones, Norm Van Lier, Bob McAdoo, and Tom McMillen, who was later elected to the House of Representatives. There was a lot of talent on the basketball court that day, so my dad and I were thrilled to be there.

"If there is a terrapin turtle on page fifty-six of your program," the announcer called out over the loudspeaker, "please come down at halftime to shoot from half-court and compete for an AMC Pacer."

I turned to my dad, practically jumping out of my seat. "A car?!" I couldn't believe it. I opened my program and there it was, a terrapin turtle on page fifty-six.

I was a very serious hoop player in those days, so this was a dream come true. To this day, I still hold the record for the highest career-total points for Plymouth Junior ABA Basketball in a four-year period. I made 1,084 points between 1971 and 1975. I used to average about 22 points per game. I weighed almost nothing, but boy, could I shoot the lights out of a basket. My dad was all in. He would take me to games whenever he could—at the best high schools in Philly, when the 76ers played at the old Spectrum, or when the Big 5 tournament came to the Penn Palestra. My father played on Sundays in a men's league, and we used to go with him to watch him play. He even installed the first see-through plexiglass backboard in the entire state of Pennsylvania, with a custom fabricated iron pole and bracketing system—right in our driveway. It was so big and heavy, it had to be installed with the help of a tow truck.

All the kids in the neighborhood came to our house to play ball. There was always a game on, day and night. When the neighbors complained about the noise and spotlights on in our driveway, which would sometimes go on until ten or eleven o'clock at night, my dad would say, "Listen, my kids aren't running in the streets. I know where they are. They can play hoops." Then he'd turn around and tell us, "Don't come in until you make five straight foul shots that go in with a swish." This meant the ball couldn't touch the rim; it had to be all net. No matter how long it took, my brothers and I each made our five swish shots from the foul line before heading into the house—and we had to do this every single day. It was that kind of discipline that turned all three of us into excellent ball players.

When halftime came around at the ACC finals that night in Maryland, my dad and I walked down from the bleachers and stood side court. The place was packed, and we watched several shooters ahead of me miss completely. No one got the ball even close to the foul line, let alone the rim. Even though I was tiny, I had a Stephen Curry kind of range and had been shooting half-court shots for years. I would play out scenarios in my head with five seconds left in the game and my team down by one point. I'd have the ball at half-court and would spin, dribble, and shoot to win the game. I dreamed I was Pistol Pete Maravich, my favorite player to this day. He was a prolific scorer in both college and the pros and still has the highest per season collegiate career scoring average of 44.2 points per game—and he did it in three years, because at the time, freshman could not play on varsity.

"Look," my dad said, pumping me up, "you hit these half-court shots all the time. You've got this." He patted me on the back, and I walked out to half-court.

I was methodical. I dribbled the ball to the basket and then back to half-court, ignoring the crowd. It was a leather ball; I was used to rubber outdoor balls, so I had to take a minute to get used to handling it. I looked all around at the packed field house to get my bearings. I eyed the distance of the shot and warmed up my arms. The crowd was starting to get annoyed.

"Hurry up," people shouted. "Just shoot the ball."

I could see my dad's arms go up, signaling everyone to calm down and give his son time. He had my back, as always.

Finally, I was ready. I launched the ball from half-court and could immediately see that it had the perfect spin that I'd watched a thousand times before. The basketball arched through the air across the court exactly as I'd hoped. Everything was in slow motion as we all waited to see where the ball would land. When it hit the backboard, the place erupted. It looked like a perfect shot as the ball circled around the rim like a magnet was drawing it into the basket. But then, the ball came off the front of the rim without going in the net. Even though I didn't make the basket, the crowd went crazy cheering for me. Everyone was screaming about the scrawny kid from Philly who'd almost made a basket from half-court.

My dad looked at me. He didn't say a thing, but he could feel my disappointment. *How could you miss that shot, Eric? You hit that all the time.* To be clear, he wasn't disappointed *in* me; he was disappointed *for* me. As we started to walk back toward the bleachers, he stopped me on the court, grabbed both my shoulders, and looked me square in the eyes. "Eric, you did great, son. I am proud of you." It was nice but didn't make me feel any better. I still think about that missed shot.

Whenever something important is on the line, I think to myself, *Don't miss your shot, Eric.* It has become a sort of life motto. It motivates me and reminds me to bring my A-game to everything I do. But that day, as my dad and I walked back up into the bleachers, I was disappointed and pissed off. We sat back down and quietly watched the rest of the game. My dad put his arm around my shoulder. He knew how hard I was on myself when I failed. He was always there for me. Though he was tough on all three of his sons when it came to sports, practice, and school, he always offered unconditional love. I knew I'd have to work harder to get ready for my next big opportunity. But I could also still hear all those fans cheering for me, even though I'd missed the shot. It felt good to have a moment in the spotlight, doing something I loved with my dad, away from the bullies. I'd take fans over fear any day.

CHAPTER 3

THERE'S ALWAYS
A WAY

"In the midst of every crisis, lies great opportunity."

—*Albert Einstein*

W hen I was in the eighth grade, my dad was transferred to the New York City office of his company. He couldn't afford the train fare, so he faced a two-and-a-half-hour drive each way from Philly to Manhattan. With a five-hour commute each day, you can imagine how early he had to leave in the morning and how late he got home—and this was on days when he wasn't on the road as a traveling salesman. He could have asked his family to move closer to Manhattan, but he didn't. My brothers were top students and two of the best basketball players in Philly. My oldest brother, Robbie, was up for basketball and academic scholarships from many of the top small colleges in the country. He would ultimately go to University of Pennsylvania on an academic scholarship. He believed he would go further with an Ivy League education than by playing hoops in college. My middle brother, Richie, would go to University of Vermont and become a Truman Scholar. Giving their kids the best education possible was always a priority for my parents. Both my parents and grandparents believed education could inoculate us against antisemitism. In the minds of my parents, there was just too much at stake to move us from Philly to New York City. It was a good example of parents putting their needs aside for the good of their children.

To make matters worse, my dad's new boss was a major bully. His last name was Kreitzer. Every night when my dad got home after his long commute, you could see he'd been verbally beaten down by Kreitzer again. It was a real-life Willy Loman, *Death of a Salesman*, story. The pain and exhaustion on my dad's face was palpable. Here was this good, hardworking family man who coached us, built us up, gave us as many opportunities as he could afford, and inspired us to do more and do better—and he was being slowly torn apart by this bully in Manhattan. Kreitzer would berate my dad for *everything*. It got to all of us. It certainly got to me. My mother tried to build him up, but Kreitzer would just push him back down every day.

My mom also worked, as a secretary for local newspaper called *Today's Post*. But even with two incomes, money was always tight. Dad and Mom promised us two gifts every year: a new basketball for our birthdays and new sneakers for Hannukah. The rest of their money would pay for a roof over our heads, basketball leagues, food on the table, and our education. After that, there wasn't much money left. Vacations were either a week with my Aunt Rosella in Pennsauken, New Jersey, or a long drive to my grandparents' apartment in Miami, Florida—and stopping in Daytona Beach on the way down. But I was just a kid, so my parents' lack of money didn't stop me from wanting things. In the summer of 1974, when I was twelve, I wanted one thing *really* bad. I wanted to go to Comet Trails Basketball Camp in Cumberland, Maryland. The camp was run by powerhouse coaches Tony Zanin of Haverford College and Ernie Prudente of Swarthmore College. These schools were known for two things—strong academics and great basketball. Additionally, I idolized Dickie Voight, a swashbuckling shooting guard with long hair and amazing ballhandling and shooting skills who played for a small but well-known basketball school called Textile College in Philadelphia. He was a rebel, and boy, could he shoot! Once I found out he was going to be a counselor at the Comet Trails camp, I wanted in *bad*. In addition, several well-known pro basketball players such as Wes Unseld and Mike Riordan from the then Baltimore Bullets would come and speak to the campers. Voight's coach, Herb Magee, also known as the Shot Doctor, was one of the winningest college basketball coaches of all time. He was going to be running the shooting clinics. I had to go. I just had to.

"Dad, *please* can I go to Comet Trails Basketball Camp. *Please!*"

"I'm sorry, Clyde. Money is too tight right now. Robbie's in college, and Richie's going soon. Why don't you call Coach Zanin and see what he can do? Or maybe you can cut a few extra lawns this spring or save more money from your newspaper delivery route."

My dad called me Clyde after Clyde Kaddidlehopper from the old Red Skelton comedy TV show, and was referring to my newspaper delivery route, which I ran from 5:00 to 6:30 a.m. every weekday morning and then again for an hour and a half in the afternoons. I knew I couldn't mow enough extra lawns or save enough money from my paper route in time to pay for the camp, so I racked my brain for a work-around. I came up with an idea when I realized that the camp brochure gave out Coach Zanin's office number. The next day, I called his office. To my surprise, his assistant put me through. Coach Zanin didn't know me from Adam, but that didn't stop me from presenting my idea.

"Hello, Coach. My name is Eric Bland. I'm twelve years old, and I want to come to your basketball camp, but my father cannot afford it." I was nervous, so I just blurted out my idea. "If I can get five of my friends to come and pay full tuition for your camp, can I come for free?"

There was a moment of quiet on the other end of the line, and my heart started racing.

"Well, Eric," Coach Zanin replied, "I think that's a wonderful idea. If you can do that, you can absolutely come for free."

So, that summer, five of my buddies and I went to the Comet Trails Basketball Camp and learned from the best. I did the same thing the following summer. If that's not a lesson in the power of determination and thinking outside the box, I don't know what is. By the age of twelve, I'd discovered firsthand that there's always a way if you work hard, believe in yourself, and get creative when confronted with a problem. Don't take no for an answer. Figure it out. I have lived my whole life thinking outside the box, getting creative, and patching together work-arounds. If you have a goal or a dream, make it happen.

*   *   *

Basketball opened a lot of doors for me. When I turned fourteen, it provided an opportunity for me to attend a prestigious private school, Chestnut Hill Academy, with a reduced tuition. My middle brother was a star basketball player there, so I was considered based on his reputation as a good student and hoops player. Not only was I one of only two or three Jewish kids at the school, but I was from a very different side of town. The wealthiest families in Philly sent their kids to Chestnut Hill Academy. It was a rigorous academic institution, and I was coming from a public school, so it was recommended that I repeat ninth grade, which I did. Still, I made friends easily because of my big mouth and hoop skills, despite the awkward economic disparities. I lived in an 1,800-square-foot home in the modest Plymouth Meeting neighborhood about forty minutes from campus. My new best friend, Stefan Karnavas, lived in the prestigious Germantown neighborhood in a 20,000-square-foot home built in the 1920s on six acres of land. My dad was a traveling salesman, while Stefan's father was chief legal counsel for the pharmaceutical behemoth Smith, Kline & French. While I didn't experience the physical bullying I had experienced in elementary school, I was regularly shamed for my family's lack of wealth by some of the richer, smarter students I was not close with.

My mother and father sacrificed everything to give me a top-notch, private-school education. But unlike my high-achieving brothers, I was a horrible student and a pain in the ass in class. I squandered most of the opportunities my parents offered me. Yep, I was the goof-off, the prankster, the class clown—and I was always in trouble. One time, a group of us came up with the idea to put the Spanish teacher's Volkswagen on cinder blocks so he'd get in his car, press the gas pedal, and go nowhere. We pulled it off, and his wheels spun and spun while we all laughed our heads off. It was a group effort, but I got blamed for it. This happened a lot. On another occasion, three other students snuck off campus with me to Dalessandro's Steaks and Hoagies in Manayunk for lunch. It's one of the best cheesesteak shops in all of Philadelphia. We sat in my car, ate our lunch, and drank two or three beers each, which we'd picked up at a convenience store with fake IDs. Someone dared us to return to school, so on the way back, I drove my white 1967 Ford Falcon over the golf course green at the private and very exclusive Philadelphia Cricket and Country Club. I had a wild streak and would do just about anything on a dare. It was always about entertaining and impressing my friends. Being a reckless daredevil was my immature way of overcompensating for my small stature.

This meant that when my dad walked in the house after a long day as Willy Loman, I'd have to say, "Hi, Dad. You've got to call Mr. Boyer. He needs to talk to you." Mr. Boyer was head of the middle and upper schools at Chestnut Hill Academy. Due to all my troublemaking, we'd gotten to know each other quite well. My dad would have to take off work the next morning for yet another meeting about his son's classroom shenanigans and campus-related issues. I felt bad, but I hated school. In the middle of my tenth-grade year, after being suspended a number of times, Chestnut Hill Academy suggested to my father that I should leave. It was a nice way of saying, "You can voluntarily pull your kid out of our institution, or we will expel him." I was headed back to public school.

This is basically when my parents gave up any remaining aspirations that I would become a decent student, let alone someone who would continue with education after high school. They didn't give up on me in a "we don't love you" sort of way. They always made me feel loved no matter what trouble I'd gotten into. It was more of a "we're exhausted and not going to fight you about school anymore" sort of way. They'd invested years of effort and care, but now faced the stark reality of their children's divergent paths: two sons had fulfilled their lofty expectations, embarking on careers they deemed prestigious and lucrative, while the third seemed destined for what they narrow-mindedly viewed as a less ambitious future. I was so different than my brothers that there was a family joke that I'd been switched at birth.

After I'd settled into Plymouth Whitemarsh High School, a monster 4A-division high school, things continued to spiral downward. Again, I made friends easily. A group of us started breaking into people's garages on weekends and drinking a lot of Genesee Cream Ale. One day, we actually broke into a house to grab some food and beer from the fridge. I felt like we were crossing a line and didn't want to do it, but I wasn't strong enough to say no or walk away from the situation. I didn't like the feeling. I kept thinking, *This is crazy. What are you doing, Eric?* But I kept doing it.

I got an after-school job at a catalog store called Basco's. My boss in the warehouse was a great guy named Dave Johnston. He was short and only weighed about 150 pounds but had impressive biceps with tattoos. I confided in him that I'd been bullied most of my childhood, and he invited me to work out with him at the nearby Landsdowne YMCA, which he did every night after work. At the time, I was only 5'7" and weighed 130 pounds. This meant I was not going to be tall enough, strong enough, or heavy enough to continue playing basketball at Plymouth Whitemarsh High School. Dave's invite was a lifeline. During our first workout, I could barely lift the bars—but I was hooked instantly. Dave told me that lifting would be my ticket out of being bullied.

"Get bigger," he said. "Get stronger. Then they'll leave you alone."

Finally, I thought, *my small body is going to match my big mouth.*

Dave was right, and from the age of sixteen onward, I never looked back. Lifting weights became one of my most important daily rituals—a central part of my life. I attacked the gym with a vengeance five days a week and ate like there was no tomorrow. Multiple PB&J sandwiches and two or three weight-gain shakes with protein powder were inhaled throughout the day. No one else in my family lifted, so they didn't really understand my obsession. This was the late 1970s, before the health and fitness craze began in the 1980s. I started to wear tighter shirts to show off my pumped muscles. By the time I was going into twelfth grade, I could bench-press 225 pounds, much more than my friends. I felt powerful and in control for the first time.

In the beginning, I didn't know how to handle my new strength. After being bullied for most of my childhood, I was now big enough to be a bully myself. All too often, those who have been bullied then bully others. It's a vicious cycle, and for a short time, I got caught up in that cycle. One day in particular haunts me. I was part of a group of boys who taped a small kid named John Tetter naked to a locker-room shower head and turned on the water. He was just like me before I started bodybuilding. He couldn't have weighed more than 90 pounds. The image of him hanging there naked while everyone laughed still makes me cringe. I went along with the crowd again—a big mistake. I might have been physically strong, but I was still emotionally immature. Even today, the fact that I did this to another human still just eats me up. I want to publicly say I'm sorry about what I did to you, John. You didn't deserve to be treated like that.

It was the last time I'd ever bully a defenseless person. I still got in fights with other tough guys, but there was no more bullying. In fact, from that day forward, if I saw someone bullying a defenseless person, someone smaller than them, I'd jump in immediately. "Why don't you pick on me instead?" I'd say. As a human, I was making progress. I was trying to close the door on a difficult part of my life. I made sure to let everyone who had bullied me know that I was no longer a skinny, defenseless kid. Later in life, I ran into Jimmy Colson at a bar and let him know—in no uncertain terms—that I was now bigger, stronger, and tougher than he was, and I threw a hard punch. To this day, it remains one of the most gratifying moments of my life.

*　　*　　*

My good friend Nick Smith told me he was planning to sign up for the Navy after graduation. I was thinking about it too. I thought it might be a way out of the mess I'd gotten myself into in high school. Nick even got a tattoo, so he'd be ready for the military. Of course, this meant I wanted one too, and by the end of the year, I had three—one on each of my calves and one on my shoulder. This was the 1980s, and tattoos were not in vogue yet. I'd hinted to my dad that I wanted a tattoo, and he'd begged me not to get one, so I hid them carefully with shirts and tube socks for the better part of a year. But one day, my grandfather Jack got a glimpse of one of my calf tattoos, and I watched his entire body recoil.

He grabbed my shoulders. "Eric, do you know what you have done to your body?" His voice was shaking.

I shrugged, not understanding his concern.

"You know Jews were tattooed during the Holocaust. The Nazis branded Jews like cattle. So, you understand why we don't believe in tattoos, right? You are spitting in the face of all the Holocaust survivors and your heritage."

I worshipped my grandfather but still didn't care. I was just a kid, unconcerned with history. I just wanted to be cool. Unfortunately, this would be one of our last conversations. The complex events of his death are still seared in my brain.

My grandfather Jack was a tough, fearless, hardworking man well into his seventies. My mother, who's pretty tough herself, was always scared of him. He owned more than two hundred dilapidated row houses in Philadelphia, but he suffered from kidney disease and underwent dialysis three days a week for six hours. These treatments never stopped him from driving over to the row houses to collect rent from his tenants. As a slumlord, he was targeted by Philadelphia mayor Bill Green, along with four others, for a slew of housing violations. He told my mother not to worry about the criminal charges that were coming. He would figure it out.

He was right, but not in the way he'd imagined.

A few days before my grandfather Jack was going to be criminally charged, he was driving to the hospital for his dialysis. He stopped at a traffic light along the way and must have watched in horror as the trailer of a large semitrailer truck detached and barreled down the hill directly toward him. He and his car were crushed, and he died at the hospital that day.

I still remember the police coming to our house to arrest my grandfather. At first, I don't think the police believed my parents when they said my grandfather had died the day before. Maybe the officers thought my grandfather was trying to dodge the law. But after a bit of back-and-forth, they finally accepted the news and left. It was frightening and sad. My beloved grandfather Jack was an alleged criminal, and now he was dead—and I'd made him miserable with my stupid tattoos. The voice inside my head was getting louder, and it was saying, *Eric, you need to right the ship before it's too late.* Like my grandfather, my parents were heartbroken when they found out about my tattoos. I was starting to care. I was beginning to feel regret about my actions and how they were impacting the people I loved—not enough to change yet, but enough to start feeling some remorse and guilt.

* * *

Another moment of searing clarity happened during my senior year of high school in 1980. I was in my bedroom one evening, goofing off, when I heard my mom crying in the kitchen. My dad had just arrived home from his grueling daily commute to New York—and dealing daily with Kreitzer. Quietly, I walked over to the stairs and sat on the blue shag carpet halfway down. I peeked through the railings. Over to the right, I saw my parents sitting at the kitchen table. My mom was bawling.

"Howard, what are we going to do?"

"I don't know, but they gave me one month's severance. Don't worry, Mollie, I'll figure it out."

"What do you mean *figure it out*? Robbie's at Penn, and Richie's at University of Vermont. How are we going to pay for them to finish college? How are we going to live?"

"I don't know yet, but I'll figure it out."

My dad's elbows were on the table, and I saw him plant his face into his hands. He was a broken man. He'd worked for Plicose for the last five years and spent the last two and a half years doing that hellish commute to face his bully of a boss day in and day out. Sitting there alone on the stairs, tears running down my cheeks, I was filled with emotions—regret, anger, sorrow, outrage, fear, and helplessness. I felt my father's anguish as the gravity of his termination struck me. Despite doing good, hard work and traveling for his company for five years, he was being let go. It didn't seem fair or right. I was also ashamed for all of the bullshit I'd put my parents through. I felt like a total failure as their son.

I'm sorry I'm such a fuckup, Dad. I'm sorry I'm disappointing you and making your life harder.

But I also wondered, *Dad, why did you let them do this to you—to us? Why didn't you leave that asshole of a boss and get another job? Why didn't you stand up for yourself and be more assertive?*

I promised myself right then and there that nobody would ever do this to me. Nobody! Ever! I wouldn't let them. I would control my own destiny! In that moment, I learned that hard work and good results often are not enough. It also taught me that you have find your "hook" to make yourself unique and somewhat indispensable.

Not only would my parents' heart-wrenching conversation shape my future career choices, but my dad's next job would ultimately become my connection to South Carolina—that's right, home of Alex Murdaugh. It's one reason I've come to believe that every challenge has a purpose, even if you don't understand it at the time. A colleague whom my dad had put in the business, Dan Williamson, had started his own company, Dan F. Williamson and Co., in Greenville, South Carolina. Dan was a great guy, and I had met him in Philadelphia once. He was a bear of a man and a collegiate football official for ACC games on the side. He generously offered my father minority owner-ship in his business, which he said my father could purchase over time. Though the move from Philadelphia to Greenville would be a significant culture shock for my family, Dan's offer was a godsend that allowed my parents to avoid financial ruin and keep my brothers in college, where they were both thriving.

* * *

On my eighteenth birthday in 1980, before my grandfather Albert died, I woke up early and found him in the kitchen. He gave me a big hug while I rubbed the sleep out of my eyes.

"Happy birthday, Eric. Don't you have somewhere to be?"

I shrugged my shoulders as I poured some coffee. "Where, Pop-Pop?"

"The post office. You're eighteen now. You need to register for the selective services." He was smiling ear to ear but was 100 percent serious.

All four of my grandparents loved America. They were so appreciative of the wonderful life it had given them. It was a haven in a violent, turbulent, and troubled world. My grand-father knew I had plans to enlist in the Navy. He also knew I'd applied to colleges, but mostly to keep my parents off my back. Luckily, I was going to graduate from high school—even if just barely. I had a C average. I also had extremely low standardized test scores. I didn't take a prep course or prepare. I just didn't care. I knew my very low SAT score would prevent me from get-ting into college, so in my mind, the application process was an exercise in futility. But by some miracle, I got into a local com-munity college and the University of Tampa in Florida, which I had applied to for two reasons that had nothing to do with aca-demics. First, the place sounded like paradise. Who wouldn't want to go to college near the Clearwater beaches? Second, I wanted to get as far away from my childhood as possible. And if I'm being honest, I felt like such a disappointment to my parents that I needed space from them.

My uncle Alvin, another of my family heroes, knew I'd probably choose the Navy over college. He'd been a lieutenant colonel during World War II and the Korean War and wanted to make sure I understood what my future would look like in the Navy.

He sat me down one day and said, "Eric, let me tell you what the military is like. You have no identity. You are part of a team."

I stared back at him, not sure what that meant but trying to be respectful.

"And you've got the sassiest, smart-ass mouth I've ever heard. That doesn't work in the military. You're going to find yourself battling the stockades, losing weekend privileges, and scrubbing toilets because of that mouth."

He went on to explain that my mouth, however, could be an asset outside the military. "You are a wonderful conversationalist and have great capacity to talk and listen, Eric. You should figure out how to use these skills in your life."

This made sense to me. Hearing someone I trusted who'd served in the military discouraging me from enlisting made an impact. I knew my mouth had always gotten me in trouble. It didn't take long for me to mull it over. I accepted the invitation to attend University of Tampa and was college bound.

In the end, my friend Nick went off to the Navy, and I graduated from Plymouth Whitemarsh High School in 1981 with the "Dear Abby" award because people told me their problems and I gave them advice. Maybe this foreshadowed my career in law. I didn't attend my graduation. It was meaningless to me. Instead, I drove down to Avalon at the Jersey Shore, where I'd started working as a bouncer in a bar. My friends and I partied there all summer and continued to weight lift like beasts. My two best friends at the time were Joe Messa and John Padova. Joe is now one of the top trial lawyers in Philly and president of the Philadelphia Trial Lawyers Association and has achieved many settlements in excess of $20 million. And John is a judge in Philadelphia. We ended up being a pretty successful group after we moved past the parties of our youth. But that summer, fun in the sun and then college in paradise beckoned. The future looked like one continuous party, and I didn't expect much to change in Florida. Boy, was I wrong!

CHAPTER 4

EITHER SINK OR SWIM

"It's never too late to be what you might have been."

—*George Eliot*

I n August 1981, my dad helped me pack up my 1967 Ford Falcon and sent me off to college.

"Eric, it's a straight shot. Take I-95 south and stop in Petersburg, Virginia, to stay the night. Wake up early the next morning and drive south all day. You'll make it to Tampa."

This conversation was my grand collegiate send-off.

I'd never seen the campus where I'd start my freshman year. I'm pretty sure my parents didn't drive me down because they were sure I'd flunk out and be back home soon. Ironically, my trip to Florida took me right through the state of South Carolina, as it had when I was a young kid and my family was driving to see family in Florida for vacation.

Besides the beautiful beaches and distance from my family, University of Tampa appealed to me because Frank Calta had a gym only half a mile from campus. As both Mr. Florida and a Mr. America competitor, he was a bodybuilding legend. By the time I left home, I'd been lifting for three years and weighed about 185 pounds. My goal was to be a bodybuilder in the sun, showing off my buff physique to all the girls on the beach. Class? Studying? No way. This was college. It was supposed to be fun. This was my first time away from home for an extended period. This was freedom. I couldn't have cared less about academics. The first two weeks were party central. I'd go to the gym. I'd tan by the pool. I'd meet friends at the beach. There was a lot of drinking in the campus bar called the Rathskeller, and I was having the time of my life. When week three rolled around, I still hadn't gone to a single class or even bought my books.

Then, one night, everything changed. It was a change I embraced, and it put me on a path of success that would change the trajectory of my life.

I remember my feet hitting the concrete bottom of the pool like hundred-pound weights pounding into a rock wall. My body should have shattered to pieces, but it didn't. The cool water shocked me out of my drunken stupor, and I realized I hadn't broken both my legs—or worse yet, hit my head on the concrete and died. Confused but grateful, I squatted, propelled my fully clothed body back up to the surface of the water, and swam over to the side to catch my breath. I crossed my arms and rested my chin on top of them, hugging the concrete rim of the pool like a life raft. That's when I looked up. Everybody was clapping, cheering, and throwing empty beer cans down from the balcony from which I'd jumped.

"Shit," I said out loud as I pushed back my wet hair. "Shit!"

The balcony had to be at least forty feet up and a good twenty feet away from the pool. Not only had I jumped a long way down, but I'd also pushed my pumped-up, five-ten body far enough out to traverse a terrace and huge concrete patio. Our freshman dorm, Rivershore Towers, was actually a converted, twelve-story Holiday Inn. It was posh. But clinging to the side of the pool in the dark, I was no longer aware of my surroundings. I just kept staring up at everyone partying on the balcony. I had just been there with them a few minutes ago, but I now felt a lifetime away. Several floors above the party, just beyond the building's roof, I could see a perfectly clear and starry night.

Are you out of your fucking mind? What the hell is wrong with you? You could've killed yourself! You're doing exactly what Dad, Mom, and your brothers said you'd do. You're a fuckup, and you're going to flunk out of college. Shit! They're probably taking bets on it right now. Dad is paying for you to go to a private college with major student loans, and you're such a fuckup, you're not even going to class.

I pounded my head on my crossed arms a few times. "You're an idiot. What the hell are you doing?" I whispered out loud. For the first time in my life, I had complete clarity. I knew I had a choice to make. Either I'd go back up to the party and live up to everyone's very low expectations or I'd walk away and turn things around.

My pivot was on a dime. Soaking wet, I got out of the pool and went to my dorm room to sleep off the alcohol. The next morning, I woke up early, even though my head was pounding. At the time, I was rushing a fraternity, but I took my name off the list. I went to buy my books and attended my first college class. From that day forward, I never missed a single college class. I worked my ass off. Between classes, I studied at the library. I ate all my meals in the cafeteria and went to the gym religiously. I never missed a workout. Bedtime was early. No more parties. No more dating. No more fuckups. I stopped drinking. That life was over, for good.

I'm an all-or-nothing kind of guy because I know my weaknesses. I can't go half in, or I falter. I must commit fully— no exceptions—and I did. It was sink or swim. I'd literally hit rock bottom in that pool and survived. God, was I lucky! I wasn't going to tempt fate twice. The discipline of lifting kept me on the straight and narrow for the next four years. Before graduating, I was able to achieve the holy grail of weight lifters.

I could bench-press 315 pounds, squat 405 pounds, and dead-lift 500 pounds. For the last three years of college, I trained at University Gym, which was owned by legendary powerlifter Ed Gillie. Ed took me under his wing. He got me temporary jobs being a bouncer in bars and working security at rock and roll concerts for extra money. It was at his gym that I learned powerlifting and came within the orbit of some of history's greatest powerlifters such as Mike Bridges, Anthony Conyers, Rickey Dale Crain, and Pat O'Brien. The gym is also where I met my best friend at college, John Kratsa, who started calling me "EB," a nickname that my friends still use. He was an Arnold Schwarzenegger clone majoring in biology. All we did was lift and study. We became roommates and sort of the pied pipers of the gym. We even started our own fraternity of studious bodybuilders. We called ourselves the TBDs, or TriBiDelts, which stood for triceps, biceps, and deltoids.

Thanks to Ed getting me bouncer and security gigs, I got to see some cool shows. Promoters would come to our gym and recruit the biggest guys like me to act as bodyguards at certain concerts, so I worked at a Rolling Stones concert and other big-name bands when they came to town. I was working, so I actually got paid to see these shows. It was pretty epic. When I was asked to be part of the National Football League's security team at the Super Bowl XVIII in Tampa in 1984, I got to watch the Los Angeles Raiders defeat the Washington Redskins 38–9. At the time, it was the largest margin of victory in Super Bowl history. But that didn't stop me from studying and keeping up my grade point average. I had a spiral notebook in my back pocket underneath my yellow NFL security jacket and studied during the game. I was assigned to the Raiders, who were supposed to lose. I'll never forget being in that locker room after their landslide victory. We were all screaming, and I was slapping hands and giving handshakes to players Lester Hayes, Dave Casper, Lyle Alzado, Jim Plunkett, and Cliff Branch, as well as the Raiders team owner, the famed Al Davis. It was an unbelievable, once-in-a-lifetime experience. When I finished celebrating and high-fiving everyone in the locker room, I went back to campus and kept studying.

*   *   *

Our lives are shaped by a thousand small choices. You can drink your life away or get up and do something productive. You can go to the gym or sit on the couch and play video games. You can eat a healthy meal or shove an extra piece of pizza in your mouth. You can be selfish or help others. These are the decisions that define our realities and shape our futures. I'd been making only bad decisions for the first nineteen years of my life—until that night at the pool party. After that, I made better decisions. I'm not saying it was easy, but the shift was as simple as that. I'm living proof that anyone can course correct and change their destiny. Make better decisions and life improves dramatically. Period.

Having cheated death—or at a minimum, catastrophic injury—and walked away unscathed, I began to believe that life must have more in store for me than just another drink fest. That night, holding on to the side of the pool, wet, drunk, and dazed, I'd made a conscious decision to find out what that might be—to be open to life's possibilities and do the hard work necessary to make them realities. Understandably, my parents were skeptical. I'd given them every reason to be. Our conversations during those first few months of school were tense.

"How's school, Eric?"

"You know, it's okay, Dad, I'm—"

"Are you studying?" he'd interrupt. I could hear the worry in his voice.

"Yeah, Dad, I'm studying."

"Eric, are you *studying*?"

"Yes, Dad. I promise. I'm studying."

"Are you lifting?"

"Yes, I'm lifting every day."

"Well, how are you getting your work done if you're lifting, Eric?"

"Dad, I'm lifting and getting the work done. Don't worry."

"Okay, we'll see what your grades are when you come home."

I didn't have the money to go home for Thanksgiving my freshman year, so I did not see my parents until the holiday break, after the end of my first semester. Believe it or not, I had a 4.0 GPA. To say that my family was shocked is an understatement. They were pleased, but they all wondered if it would last. I was a criminal justice major and would later take on a minor in political science because I wanted to be a Secret Service agent. Sober, healthy, and strong, I was starting to see a future for myself, even if my family was still unsure. Their disbelief only fueled my drive to succeed and achieve.

* * *

The self-discipline I developed during my four years at the University of Tampa was life altering. But it was another seminal moment during my junior year that changed the trajectory of my life. I found a lump on my throat, and it started growing and growing and growing. At its largest, it was the size of a grapefruit. When I called my dad to tell him, he said, "Eric, you have to come home."

My parents were now settled into their new life in Greenville, South Carolina, so the drive was only about eight hours. It was spring break, and I had an appointment with Dr. Mann, my parents' general practitioner. He told me the growth was either a Hodgkin's lymphoma, a life-threatening cancer of the lymph tissue, or a benign cyst. Either way, I'd have to have surgery.

The wait was excruciating. After my surgery, they tested the mass. Luckily, it turned out to be a benign cyst. We were all so relieved. After the positive prognosis, I remember thinking, *You just got another shot, Eric. God sent you a signal, but He gave you another shot. Don't waste it!* Well, I certainly wasn't going to blow it. Profoundly grateful, I started to think about how I could give back to the world.

The first semester of my senior year, I decided to intern for PDSDC, the Public Defender Service for the District of Columbia. Most of the lawyers in that division were former Supreme Court clerks who'd worked for liberal judges like William Brennan, Hugo Black, and William Douglas. They'd decided to devote their first two years working in the trenches to give back. At PDSDC, I worked for two amazing lawyers, Doug Wood and Bernie Grimm. I watched how thoroughly they practiced law, tried cases, and interacted with their clients, the police, and the prosecutors. They were so dedicated to their jobs despite the low pay and long hours. I was also impressed by how hard they fought for their clients. I remember being sent to the DC jail to interview clients and all over the city to talk with witnesses at all hours of the day and night. It was exhausting but a tremendous learning experience at all levels. There was only one problem. I didn't want to be a lawyer; I wanted to be a Secret Service agent. I was obsessed with the look of those huge guys like me in their black suits with their black sunglasses and ear gear so they could talk to each other. It was all just so cool! This was after White House Press Secretary James Brady was shot during an assassination attempt on President Ronald Reagan in 1981. I remember the Secret Service agents diving in front of the president and whisking him off to safety. It was all so heroic and inspiring. *That's* what I wanted to do. So, when I finally got my chance to interview with the Secret Service, I gave it my all.

After a couple of interviews, I sat down with a Tampa-based Secret Service officer for what would be my last interview. He looked confused as he reviewed my résumé.

"Son," he said, looking me straight in the eye, "you're going to get the job. But you don't want to work in the Secret Service." I'm sure I looked shocked, but I didn't interrupt him. "I see your grade point average. Very impressive. I've read all the letters of recommendations from your professors, and I see all the awards. Again, very impressive. So, what are you doing? You should be going to law school."

"Sir," I said respectfully. "I just want to guard the president of the United States."

He leaned back in his chair with a knowing smile. "Well, let me give you a little advice. You're not going to guard the president. You're going to end up with some retired ambassador in middle America, and you're going to be his glorified chauffeur. You're going to pick up his dry cleaning. You're going to take his kids to school. You're not cut out for that kind of job or the long wait. It takes years and years and lots of luck to get to the point where you can guard the president. That's not you. Go to law school, son."

I don't think I was allowed to even know his name. It was the Secret Service after all. But that interviewer changed my life.

"Okay," I said to this well-informed, perfect stranger. "I guess I'll go to law school then."

I would take the LSATs a few months later, after my college graduation—doubting, like always, that I'd score high enough to get in anywhere. But I did. I'd applied to University of South Carolina School of Law because my parents' residency allowed me to qualify for in-state tuition. Lo and behold, I was accepted. Maybe there would be two lawyers in the family, I thought, as my brother Richard had just graduated from law school and accepted a position as an associate with a large law firm in Burlington, Vermont.

My parents did not visit me at the University of Tampa until 1985, when I graduated number two in my class with a 3.92 grade average—*magna cum laude*. I was inducted into the

Alpha Chi National Honors Society. I only had a single B in all my thirty-seven undergraduate classes. I'd won dozens of academic awards and commendations. It had been an intense four years, but I had not only made it through, I'd thrived. I was a different person than that kid who'd driven down I-95 and walked right into a beach party. I was no longer reckless or aimless. I was an accomplished student and, more importantly, a better person. As would become my custom, I did not want to attend my college graduation ceremony—but my father would have none of it. He was so proud that I had turned my life around. He and my mother drove down from South Carolina. There was no way they were going to miss watching their son receive his diploma. Only four years earlier, the prospect of me going to college and actually graduating had been laughable. The idea that I would graduate with high honors had been unfathomable. My most vivid memory of that day is watching my parents just smile all day long.

To this day, I still have trouble being recognized for accomplishments or celebrating life's victories, even the big ones. I get restless. That voice in my head warns me not to sit still, not to get complacent, because all the good stuff might disappear. It tells me if I stop to celebrate, I might lose my momentum and my discipline. That voice in my head still wonders if I deserve the good stuff after all the shit I've done. The moment I accomplish something, I tell myself that I can do better, I can do more, and it's time to move on. Law school at the University of South Carolina awaited in the fall, and I knew I had to start preparing for my next big challenge.

CHAPTER 5

THE UNIVERSE WANTS
A POUND OF FLESH

"Mistakes are part of the dues one pays for a full life."

—*Sophia Loren*

M y best friend at law school was a Mormon with six kids. His name was Joe Connell, and he worked full-time at a local convenience store to pay his way. It was 1985, and we ran into each other on the first day of orientation at University of South Carolina School of Law. He didn't look like the other law students—who were mostly dressed in preppy, pastel, button-down cotton shirts and khakis—and I certainly didn't look like anybody else wearing my weight-lifting tees and gym shorts. It only took us a moment to recognize each other as fellow misfits. We clicked immediately and became fast friends and study mates.

Joe didn't have time to study as much as needed with his work schedule, and I was pretty sure I was going to flunk out because of everything I'd heard about law school—in addition to my constant fear of failure—so our unlikely friendship proved a gift to me. To help Joe out, I would read all the material and learn it myself. Then, I would outline everything and teach it to Joe on the weekends. As we all know, teaching is the best way to master a subject, so our arrangement helped me immensely. I lived on Pendleton Street, about a fifteen-minute walk to campus, in the tiny basement apartment of a house owned by Marvin Kaufman, a former assistant US attorney. Joe and I studied hard during the week. On the weekends, we studied even harder. We locked ourselves in on Friday night and worked like bandits until Sunday night. We didn't socialize. We didn't go out. That first year, I didn't even have a TV. We just studied our butts off.

I did keep up with my workouts. They kept me sane. Weight lifting had helped me turn my life around. Just because I was crazy busy with law school didn't mean I was going to let my fitness ritual slip away. More than ever, I needed the strength and confidence it gave me to deal with the stress of law school. I started working out with the USC football team and got to know some of the players. Soon, I was invited to become a paid tutor for some of them.

Since law school grades depend primarily on a single final exam, it's tough to judge how you're doing along the way—except for the occasional classroom eye-opener. Lucky for me, I had one of those early in my first semester, and it confirmed my worst fears. One weekday, I didn't plan things out so well and realized I'd have to wear my T-shirt and sweatpants to a law lecture after my workout. I was running a few minutes late, so all the other students had taken their seats when I rushed in looking like a muscleman coming from a weight-lifting competition. I'll never forget the glare my professor gave me. I knew he was going to eat me alive.

Law schools teach by Socratic method, which means students are not meant to receive knowledge passively. They are asked to use it in guided dialogues with their professors. In other words, ideas and the defense of those ideas are refined as one question begets another. The term *productive discomfort* has often been used to describe this classroom environment. Students are meant to feel tested, not intimidated—at least, in theory. This was not the case the day Professor James R. Burkhard saw me enter in my muscle shirt. From the moment he called my name, it was clear he was going to make an example of me—and so he did.

"Mr. Bland, please stand up."

I stood up, my physique a clear outlier among my peers, drawing curious glances from around the room. Even a suit wouldn't have been able to hide my Hulk-like physique. I was proud of my size and fitness, but at that moment, I felt like the scrawny kid who had been bullied long ago.

Professor Burkhard had a reputation of being one of USC law school's toughest professors. Heck, his last name even has the word *hard* in it! For those of you who remember the legal show *The Paper Chase*, set at Harvard University in the 1970s, Professor Burkhard reminded me of the fictional tough guy Professor Kingsfield—only this wasn't a TV series, it was my *real* life.

When Burkhard came for me, I was able to hold my own for a couple of minutes. I believe this was a result of my rigorous study of the subject matter. But the Socratic method was completely new to me. And with all his power, experience, and knowledge, Professor Burkhard tripped me up good. I was completely lost by the third minute. I'll never forget what he said as I crumbled in front of him and the entire class.

"Mr. Bland, you are obviously spending more time in the gym than at the library studying. You should probably call your parents and tell them they are wasting their money because you're not going to make it here or as a lawyer."

I stood perfectly still as his words pounded in my skull.

"Mr. Bland, you may sit down now."

I slumped in my chair and, for a brief second, panicked. *Oh, God,* I thought, *the gig's up! He is so right.* But by this point, this type of criticism wasn't new to me. I'd heard these words most of my life—and I wasn't the mess I used to be. I'd accomplished more than anyone had expected. Still, as I walked out of class, I fought back an overwhelming sense of defeat. The professor's words played in my head over and over.

"Mr. Bland, you are not going to make it . . . you are not going to make it . . . you are not going to make it . . ."

But the more I heard it, the more my defeat shifted to anger. *Who the hell is he to tell me what I can and can't do? I'm studying my ass off!* By the time I was a block from my apartment, the street fighter in me had been awakened like a great kraken emerging from its ocean lair. I was mad as hell.

"Screw him!" I said out loud.

I didn't fully understand it at the time, but Professor Burkhard's words were another gift—the rocket fuel I needed not just to survive law school but to propel myself to the top of my class. I'd prove him wrong. Yeah, I'd prove them all wrong!

Professor Burkhard taught me another important lesson that day: presentation matters. I would never show up for class in workout clothes again. Sure, I'd wear my gym clothes around campus because I didn't really care about fitting in outside the classroom. Besides, I had to work out. It was the only way I could stay mentally strong and focused enough to grind out the endless hours of study. And I certainly wasn't ever going to be preppy— so why care? But when it came to showtime in the classroom, I decided to play the part. Professor Burkhard had taught me that—right or wrong—law school professors absolutely judged a book by its cover. Impressions matter!

*   *   *

Thanks in part to the academic beast Professor Burkhard had awakened, I not only survived my first year of law school but finished in the top 10 percent of my class. As a result, I was able to land a pretty prestigious legal clerkship at a Philadelphia law firm called Cozen O'Connor. Law firms treat student clerks like royalty. It's a form of courting. If you have a great experience, and if they like you, the lawyers know you're likely to come work for them. Of course, once you are extended an offer to be an associate and sign on the dotted line, your life becomes theirs and they work you to the bone—but you don't know that when you're clerking during your first summer in college, so you just enjoy the ride and hope they like you. Not only do you put your best foot forward as a smart and hardworking clerk, but you also try to fit in. Only a handful of clerks get job offers, so you try to impress on a personal and professional level. You also try to be friendly with the other clerks, even though you know they're the competition.

All the clerks were a bit nervous, but we also had a lot of fun. The firm took us to Philly's games, nice restaurants for lunches, outdoor symphonies, dinners, and clerk parties. Cozen O'Connor spared no expense to show us a good time after work. At the end of the summer, as we all prepared to head back to law school, one of the partners invited us to his house for a cookout and pool party with the whole firm. It would have been a great end to a wonderful summer, especially on a hot August evening in Philly, except for one thing. In swim trunks, I didn't look like any of the other guests, a reality that was about to become crystal clear.

I remember everything like a movie scene. The place was an early 1900s Tudor home on the famed main line of Philadelphia. Everyone was chatting it up in their designer-label bathing suits and setting down their cocktails to jump in the pool. It was a sea of slender, fit, academically successful young people trying to impress a bunch of professional suits, who in turn were trying to look natural without their business attire. The tension of this professional event masked as a leisure activity was electric and palpable. Everyone was pretending to be confident and relaxed, but we were all sizing one another up. You had to watch what you said, and you felt the eyes on you from all angles, watching how you moved and interacted. The clerks were looking for signs they would be one of the chosen few to get a job offer after law school. And the lawyers and partners were on a mission to select those chosen few. The clerks were all trying to be smart, sophisticated, and likeable—to make it into the "in" crowd—while the lawyers and partners enjoyed imparting deathblows with smiles.

"Lovely to talk with you. Well, I'd better refresh my drink and find my wife."

If you heard this type of phrase, you were out—and you didn't even see it coming.

I wasn't drinking, but like everyone else, I was trying to fit in. I decided to take off my shirt and dive into the pool. As I made my way to the pool, I couldn't help but notice the subtle shift in the room's atmosphere, my weightlifter's physique standing out in the crowd. And then there were the tattoos—one on my shoulder and one on each of my calves. The whole party suddenly hushed like a red neon sign was flashing over my head saying, "Outsider! Outsider!" None of the attorneys or partners could hide their surprise—or, honestly, their disgust. I could see that my fellow law clerks were also in shock. I could practically hear their thoughts and laughter. *Oh, yeah, this guy's definitely out. Just look at him! Tattoos—are you kidding? Nope, we don't need to worry about him getting an offer.*

I was mortified.

Sinking to the bottom of the pool—just as I had so many years earlier as a freshman in Florida—my mind wandered. *Maybe Professor Burkhard was right. Even if I get the grades and graduate, I'll never belong, I'll never fit in.* All my insecurities washed over me. I couldn't breathe. I felt myself drowning in doubt. *Just face it—you're a Jewish bodybuilder with tattoos from the blue-collar side of Philly! You'll never be a lawyer.*

I left the party and the clerkship mortified, feeling once again like a misfit sent home with my tail between my legs. I had to confront the fact that my tattoos were going to be a hinderance as I embarked on a professional career in law. In the 1980s, tattoos were not mainstream like they are today. There were a couple of weeks left of my clerkship before the start of my second year, so I headed home to see my family. My older brother Robbie's wife, Stacey, came with me to visit my parents in Greenville. We had a great time, but underneath all the catch-up chatter, I was quietly obsessed with a secret mission.

One evening when my parents were out, I cornered Stacey in the upstairs den. We were as close as any brother and sister— and I wouldn't have dared ask anyone else in my family for help with the mission I was about to share with her. All I knew was that it had to be done—and fast.

"Stacey, I want the tattoo on my shoulder off."

"Off? What do you mean?"

"Well, I'm going downstairs to remove it. I can do it myself, or you can help me."

I watched her assess my expression. She must have decided I was serious because she reluctantly motioned toward the stairs. We rummaged around the kitchen until we found a serrated knife, and I went to the garage to get some sandpaper—and a six-pack of Genesee Cream Ale.

We went down to the basement and sat at a table facing each other. She stared me right in the eyes and took a long, deep breath.

"Are you ready?"

"Not yet." I proceeded to slam back four of the six cans of the Genesee Cream Ale, one after the other. I hadn't had a drop of alcohol in more than five years.

"Yep, now I'm ready," I gasped, slamming down the last can of ale on the table.

I picked up a piece of sandpaper and started sanding the tattoo on my shoulder. We would intermittently wipe rubbing alcohol on the spot in an effort to stave off infection. It wasn't so bad at first, but as the top layers of my skin started to come off, the pain became excruciating. No matter. Nothing was going to stop me. We kept sanding and sanding and sanding. It took about thirty minutes to get to the deep layer of skin where the ink of the tattoo sat. Then, we used the serrated knife to cut out what was left. Blood was spurting out everywhere, and soon it was clear we weren't going to be able to stop it. We attempted to use ice and pressure. I even tried medical glue. I was lucky my shoulder didn't get infected, and I walked away from the entire grim affair relieved.

But I still had a problem: the tattoos on the sides of both of my calves. I figured I could hide them under long pants, and when I wore shorts, I could wear tube socks, which were in style in the 1980s. I told myself that I would have to actually seek the services of medical personnel to get these two removed because they were larger, and I didn't want to have the scarring I had where we'd crudely removed my shoulder tattoo. The following winter, the opportunity to revisit my tattoo problem presented itself. Wiser, but still undeterred, I reached out to my older brother Robbie, Stacey's husband, to ask him if he could approach his friend Dr. David Goodkind, who was a plastic surgeon, for a favor. I was hoping for the "family" discount to remove my remaining tattoos. Dr. Goodkind lived in Woodbridge, Connecticut, right outside of Yale Hospital in New Haven and had a practice there. I was still clerking at Cozen O'Conner in Philly over the winter holiday of my second year of law school, so I was able to drive up to New Haven on a Saturday and meet with Dr. Goodkind. This was before laser tattoo removal had become available, so Dr. Goodkind showed me something akin to a deli meat slicer to remove my tattoos. You really can't make this stuff up! This circular contraption, he explained, would be bracketed to my legs, and he would slowly crank it lower and lower so it could slice off one layer of skin and one layer of my tattoos at a time. I told myself it was better than a serrated knife and sandpaper, but not by much. Additionally, Dr. Goodkind was clear that he was only doing this procedure as a favor to my brother, so there would be no nurses on standby and no general anesthesia. It would be just the two of us and a local shot to somewhat numb my calves.

"I'm not going to sugarcoat it, Eric," he said. "This is going to hurt like hell, and it will be a tough road healing."

Boy, was he was right. When all was said and done, he'd probably sliced off about a quarter inch of skin from both my calves. I still have the indents. He cleaned and wrapped each wound tightly with sterile bandages and sent me on my way. It was tough to walk in the beginning. Each step was like shooting daggers. Dr. Goodkind had not offered me any painkillers, so I just had to grin and bear it.

I still had to finish a few final days of clerking before heading back to law school for the second semester of my second year. I tried to muddle through without drawing attention to my predicament. But that quickly became impossible. That Monday, the first day back after my Saturday "surgery," I was walking down the hall and felt a squishing in my socks and shoes. I looked down and saw blood gushing out of both my calf wounds and pouring down to my ankles. This bleeding went on for a month, even after I got back to University of South Carolina. It had been a grueling process, but I was finally tattoo free. I still have some ink remnants on my calves, which can be seen if you look closely. They serve as a good reminder of some of the mistakes of my youth.

The universe had demanded a pound of flesh for my rash teenage decision to get tattoos. I'd now paid that price in full—quite literally—and with no regrets. Even without the tattoos, I knew I'd never look like the average lawyer because of the weight lifting—but I was fine with that. In fact, I was getting more comfortable in my role as an outsider—maybe even starting to learn how to use it to my advantage. But I'd never again be the freak show I was at that pool party. I wanted to stand out for my skills and intelligence, not my looks.

CHAPTER 6

NEVER WAIT FOR LUCK

"Believe you can and you're halfway there."

—*Theodore Roosevelt*

The fall of 1987 was the beginning of my third and final year of law school. It was time to start looking for a job. I wanted to go back to Philly. I hadn't yet warmed to the idea of spending the rest of my life in South Carolina, and I didn't think South Carolina had warmed to me either. But the Northern firms weren't recruiting from USC. All the law firm recruiters who were visiting the school, setting up job fair booths, and interviewing third-year USC law students were from the south—Charlotte, Raleigh, Atlanta, Charleston, Columbia, and so forth. I was lucky; I'd worked my ass off and stayed in the top 10 percent of my class and was on track to receive top academic honors at graduation, including the Order of the Wig and Robe. This meant I could have any interview I wanted. But I didn't want any of them—I wanted to go home to Philly.

Feeling a bit desperate, I went to see Sharon Williams. As the law school's placement coordinator, Sharon was a very important person on campus.

"Sharon, I really want to work in Philly. Could you help me out and make some intros?"

She was a nice woman and competent professional.

"Eric, the reality is USC has no connections with law firms up north. We just don't. Occasionally, the top graduate will get an offer from a big New York law firm, but even that's pretty rare. I'm sorry I can't be of more help. I'll try my best, but don't get your hopes up."

It was a big setback. I'd have to make cold calls and form connections on my own. This would not be easy in a tight-knit profession that relies on its social network for recommendations. My family was in the middle class. We were not part of the larger business or legal community in any city. Connections drove the recruiting process, and mine were limited, so I knew it would be a tough road. To get the lay of the land, Sharon suggested I go to the law library and consult *Martindale-Hubbell*, the leading directory of law firms across the country. I wrote letters and sent my résumé to the hiring coordinators at dozens of big East Coast law firms in Philadelphia and New Jersey. I even included Atlanta, Georgia, and Florida on my list. I waited for responses, but nothing came. Crickets! I needed to create some buzz.

After a couple of frustrating weeks, I decided to start calling the hiring coordinators at the law firms where I'd sent my résumé. After a number of failed connections, I finally lucked out and got the assistant of the hiring partner from the Philadelphia law firm of Wolf, Block, Schorr & Solis-Cohen on the phone. She was a nice woman, and we hit it off immediately. We talked about our favorite places, bars, and restaurants in Philly. I told her that I'd keep calling until she put me through to her boss and that I would bring her a gift if I got an interview. She finally relented and told me to call the next day at 11:00 a.m. and she would put me through to the hiring partner. As instructed, I called and was put through to the hiring partner. His initial comments to me were polite but not encouraging. He was commenting on my résumé but without enthusiasm. He said most of the larger urban firms in Philadelphia hired from Ivy League law schools. He didn't know much about the University of South Carolina School of Law. In the middle of our conversation, I decided to bet on myself with a little white lie.

"I just wanted to make you aware," I embellished, "that I have an interview at Morgan, Lewis & Bockius next Thursday at 2:00 p.m. So, I'm already in your area. If you'd like to interview me, I'm still open on Thursday morning."

Upon hearing this, his tone changed completely.

"Really? Morgan, Lewis . . ." he paused. "Hold on for just a moment. Let me check again and see if we have any openings while you're in the area."

After a minute, he came back on the line. "I actually *do* have an opening on Thursday at 10:00 a.m. Can you make that time work while you're here?"

I pretended to check my calendar and then told him yes. With that single breakthrough, I was off to the races. On the next call, I didn't have to tell a white lie because I did in fact have an interview at Wolf, Block, Schorr & Solis-Cohen. Within three calls, it was clear that this was the secret sauce to landing interviews. I created my network out of thin air. I just told one powerful law firm that I had an appointment with another powerful law firm, particularly a big competitor, and interest was immediate.

Today, I wear a bracelet that says, "Whatever It Takes," meaning do whatever it takes to get the job done, get your foot in the door, or achieve your goals. Use your mouth, your accomplishments, your friends, your relationships—just find the hook that gets you in. Once you're in, though, that's when the rubber hits the road. All your skills, knowledge, experience, and hard work will be what keep you there. I was able to parlay these conversations into four interviews with four of the top-tier Philadelphia law firms for the following Thursday and Friday. Two of the firms even offered to contribute to my travel and lodging expenses. All the interviews went very well, but my lack of an Ivy League degree was still an impediment. I wondered if this same trick would work for actual job offers—so I gave it a try.

After a forty-five-minute interview, the recruiter at Wolf, Block, Schorr & Solis-Cohen said, "Eric, it has been a pleasure getting to know you. We think you have a great future ahead of you in law, but we're not sure you're a fit here. As you know, we usually don't take associates from law schools like the University of South Carolina. We wish you the best of luck."

"I appreciate the time, sir," I said politely, standing up and shaking the man's hand. "It's fine. I've already received an offer from Fox Rothschild."

This was not true, but what did I have to lose?

"Really? You have an offer from Fox Rothschild?"

"I do, sir." I continued to move toward the door as I shared my news. "Again, thank you for your time."

"Eric, if Fox Rothschild sees something in you, perhaps we've overlooked something."

This was my opportunity to pounce.

"Yes, sir," I said, dripping with decorum as I turned back to face my interviewer. "I'm not like the other associate law candidates you've met. I grew up in a middle-class family. I know what I want, and I'll work very hard to get it. I will make you a lot of money. I will make you look good. *Nothing* will deter me from becoming a top lawyer at your firm."

At this point, I walked to the door and turned back without saying another word. I just stood there waiting for the interviewer to speak.

"Eric, tell you what, let me go back and take one more look at everything. I'll let you know if we change our mind."

"Sure. Sounds great," I said with a confident smile as I walked out the door. In the end, I turned zero interviews into twelve job offers from some of the biggest law firms on the East

Coast: Steel Hector & Davis, Shea & Gould, Gunster Yoakley in West Palm Beach, Hannoch Weisman in New Jersey, and a number of top Philadelphia firms such as Stradley, Ronon, Stevens & Young, among others.

Ultimately, I chose Wolf Block, which at the time was the largest of all the Philadelphia-based law firms. Not only were they in my hometown, but they offered me the most money— $62,500 a year and a $10,000 signing bonus. In 1988, this was *big* money, especially for kid whose father had never even made $40,000 a year in his entire career! Not only would I be able to afford a nice lifestyle, but I could also pay my dad back for the ten-year, interest-free loan he'd given me to cover my law school tuition and living expenses. He'd taken out a bank loan to do this for me. He'd been making these types of sacrifices and bets on his children his whole life. How could I let him down? I was thrilled to pull off a miracle and land the job of my dreams.

* * *

I was never one to rest on my laurels, but having a good job lined up did take some weight off my shoulders. I could finally relax a little at school and enjoy myself. One night, a few months before graduation, my friend Andrew Kornish, who I'd met through tutoring football players and weight lifting, and I decided to go to synagogue together for Friday night services. Ironically, Andrew would become a client of mine many years later. He would also convert to Christianity and become a Lutheran minister. But that night, back in the 1980s, we were just two Jewish boys going out to dinner after synagogue. We headed over to a restaurant called Pugs in Five Points, a popular bar area near campus. I was on top of the world. I had a topflight job waiting for me, and I was about to become a full-fledged lawyer. As I mentioned earlier, my older brother Richard was a lawyer. He was very smart, and no one thought I could match his achievements. But I actually landed a better job than he did. I felt great, and the minute we walked into the bar, things got even better. We saw two beautiful, dark-haired young women sitting at a table alone.

"Andrew," I whispered, "those girls are from up north. They're not blonde, and one of them is wearing a leather jacket."

We both smiled in the direction of their table. After a few minutes of long-distance flirting, they waved us to come over and join them. The first girl, whose name was Amy, had a mild Southern accent. She introduced her friend to us as Renée, who quietly nodded. The first girl was doing most of the talking so I was facing her. She mentioned she was dating Matt McKernan, the starting linebacker for USC at the time.

"We know Matt," I chimed in. "We both work out with the football team. I'm also a tutor for some of the players. Of course, Matt doesn't need any tutoring. He's a bright guy."

As we continued talking, I looked to my right at Renée, who was quietly listening to all of us. *Okay*, I thought. *Yeah, she's definitely from Jersey or Philly.*

Then Renée opened her mouth to say something, and out rolled the sweetest, thickest Southern drawl I'd ever heard. Nope, she was definitely *not* from the North. But to my surprise, it didn't matter. I was completely mesmerized by every Southern word Renée spoke. She told me she was from a small South Carolina town called Greenwood, and she was quite clear that she had a boyfriend. I was not deterred. She was gorgeous!

After an hour of great conversation and undeniable chemistry, I said with confidence, "Renée, you may have a boyfriend, but by the end of the night, you're going to give me your number." Yeah, it was cocky, but I was still riding the high of my job offer miracle. Why break the streak?

Sure enough, after a few hours of talking and dancing down the street at Sharkey's, Renée gave me her phone number. A couple of days later, I called and asked her out for dinner. Even though she had a bad cold, she said she'd come out with me for a while. We went to Villa Tronco, a little gem of an Italian restaurant in downtown Columbia and sat in a cozy booth where we talked the night away. Then, we went to see *Fatal Attraction*, neither of us realizing how racy the movie was. But all in all, it was a great evening, and from that day forward, we were inseparable. During the date, Renée told me she had been drifting away from her boyfriend. Meeting me, she said, had provided her with the impetus to end that relationship. It was a whirlwind romance. Ironically, both of us told our parents after the first date that we'd met someone special.

It didn't take long for me to realize I was falling in love. The only problem was I was leaving soon to take my dream job in Philly. By May, a month before I had to leave Columbia for good, I realized I couldn't live without her. The only way to keep the love of my life and the job of my dreams was to marry Renée. But back then, it was no small thing for a Jewish boy from Philly to propose to a Christian girl from South Carolina. Both sets of parents had concerns.

"Is she Jewish?" was my mom's first question after I told her I'd met someone.

We were in the kitchen, and my mom was chopping vegetables with her back to me. Even as an adult bodybuilder who towered over my mother, I remember being afraid to answer.

I inhaled and responded quickly on the exhale. "No, she is not, Mom."

Her back was to me, and I couldn't see her expression, but I watched her entire body deflate.

She didn't turn to face me, but after a moment of silence, she simply said, "Eric, remember when you were a teenager, you made a promise to me."

She was right. I'd promised my mom that I'd marry in the faith. It was very important to her. As a practicing Jew who loved his parents and his faith, I didn't need to hear another word. I just needed to be straightforward with Renée—even though the prospect of losing her absolutely terrified me.

At dinner with Renée a few nights later, I mustered up the courage to start the conversation. I was too nervous for a warm-up, so I just blurted it out.

"Renée, the only way I can marry you is if you convert to Judaism," I rambled. "I don't want to have a mixed marriage. I've seen it, and it doesn't work well, especially for the kids. I can't—"

"Eric," she interrupted in her gentle, captivating Southern accent, "I love you. Yes, of course I'll convert. But I don't want to be Jewish just in name. I will embrace your faith. I'll immerse myself in Judaism not just for us but for our children to come."

She went on to explain that she wasn't active in the faith of her childhood. She'd been born a Baptist, but her parents had converted and become Presbyterians. She admired my commitment to my faith. I was so relieved and couldn't wait to share the news with my family. After hearing her words, I knew I had met the perfect woman.

"Mom, Renée is going to convert." I held my breath over the phone, waiting for her response. My mom is one tough cookie, so I wasn't sure what to expect.

Without hesitation, she said, "This is very good news, Eric." I could practically feel her smile coming through the phone. She gave her blessing to us as a couple, obliterating the last impediment to our marriage on my side of the family.

But Renée's parents also had concerns, especially when they learned their daughter was going to convert to Judaism and probably move away from South Carolina. Ultimately, they accepted me, but it was hard on them. As practicing Presbyterians in rural South Carolina, their faith mattered to them as much as my faith mattered to me. There were also some strong voices in her family that were against the marriage. Her grandmother had never met a Jewish person before. She probably thought I had horns and a tail—I'm not kidding. And Renée's brother felt she had disgraced the family by even considering marriage to a Jew. It was very tough on my wife, and to this day, she and her brother are estranged. Renée gave up a lot to marry me, and I will always be grateful for her sacrifice. She is tremendously courageous. She is my rock.

Armed with our parents' approval, my grandmother's exquisite European blue diamond ring, and the keys to my parents' condominium at Marlin Quay on the ocean in Garden City, I asked Renée to join me at the beach for the weekend. It was May, and the weather was gorgeous. Surely, she knew what was coming after all our deep conversations about family and kids, as well as the numerous family objections we'd overcome together. Still, I was determined to make my formal proposal at least somewhat of a surprise. On a beautiful Carolina evening, as we were strolling by the pool, I got down on one knee and asked Renée to marry me. To my sheer joy, she said yes.

*   *   *

In 1988, my new employer, Wolf Block, was not only one of the oldest and largest firms in Philly, but it was also ranked as one of the largest law firms in the world. They were expanding and had offices in a number of cities, including West Palm Beach, Florida. Instead of assigning me to work in Philly, my new bosses said they wanted me to help them build their sports law department because of my relationships with all the South Carolina football players. They believed I could parlay those relationship into connections at other universities and help talented college players negotiate the complex contracts being offered to them by professional teams as well as the corresponding marketing opportunities. It sounded amazing to me, as long as my new fiancée could come with me.

To our amazement, Renée's very Christian parents gave us permission to live together even though we weren't married.

The wedding was planned for November, but back in 1988, this was still a huge concession. To keep the peace, we decided not to advertise the situation to the rest of Renée's family. We packed up my car and headed to West Palm Beach. We wouldn't be starting our lives in Philly, as planned, but we didn't care because we were in love and together—and that was all that mattered.

My direct boss in this new Wolf Block endeavor was going to be a guy named Howard Shapiro—and he was the real deal. Among several big-name athletes he'd represented were Mike Schmidt, a third baseman for the Phillies, who with 537 home runs was one of the greatest baseball players of all time. He'd also represented Steve Carlton, a 300-game pitching winner for the Phillies, as well as a number of football players for the Eagles. As a huge sports and Phillies fan, this job was shaping up to be epic! I couldn't believe my good fortune. I'd be practicing law, making great money, *and* hanging out with jocks—my people. The law firm's offices were right next to the Trump towers in West Palm Beach on a gorgeous waterway filled with multimillion-dollar mansions. It was a beautiful area. With my substantial salary, Renée and I were able to rent a nice apartment in a lovely neighborhood nearby called Boca Pointe. I was studying for the Florida bar examination, the four-day test I'd have to take and pass in Tampa in July to become a licensed lawyer in the state. Florida's bar exam is one of the toughest in the country. I was nervous about it—but not the way I'd been earlier in my life. I'd paid my dues, and I'd come out of law school with a great job. I'd never live up to my own expectations—and I still don't—but I knew how to study and pass these types of tests. I'd been doing it for years, and University of South Carolina School of Law had prepared me. In between work and studying, Renée and I were having a blast going to the beach and living the relaxed Florida lifestyle. We even talked about settling down in the area, even though our families and friends were far away. Life was good. I was making more money than anyone in my family had ever made, and though I'd never splurged on anything in my life, there was a partner in my office named David Layman who was selling one of his Rolex watches. He offered it to me at a great price, so I talked it over with Renée and she told me to go for it. I paid $1,500, which was probably half the Rolex's worth, and wore it proudly for many years. When my son, Davis, had his Bar Mitzvah at thirteen, I gave it to him. He still wears it today. For me, the Rolex was a symbol that I was on a good path. It was like an anti-tattoo, and I've never regretted that purchase. But if there's one thing I've learned, it's that life is full of surprises.

Shortly after buying the watch, and the day before I would leave for Tampa to take the Florida bar exam, I went into work and was surprised to see all the Wolf Block bigwigs in from Philly. All the senior partners were in the office's main conference room, including the top lawyer in the firm, Bob Segal. I could hear them all talking loudly, maybe even arguing, though I couldn't be sure. But as I passed the conference room door, a distinct hush came from the room.

"Shit, this can't be good," I murmured quietly as I kept walking to my office. I tried to shrug off the feeling that something really bad was about to happen. For God's sake, I was only one day away from taking the bar—one day!

My door was open, and I could see Bob Segal heading my way. I knew something big was about to go down.

"Hi, Eric. How are you?" Bob said, shaking my hand as I stood to greet him.

"Good, sir," I replied, swallowing hard.

"If you could come to the conference room, we've got some news to share."

The walk from my office was only a few dozen feet, but it felt like a mile. Everyone who'd been in a heated discussion just a few minutes earlier was now sitting quietly. I sat down at one end of the long mahogany conference table, and Bob Segal sat down at the other. Every chair was filled with a solemn-looking lawyer trying not to make eye contact with me. I looked at Howard Shapiro and his partner, Howard Bregman, and they looked away.

My mind was frantically trying to put the pieces of this mystery together. *I couldn't have made a mistake this big,* I thought. *I don't even have my law license yet! Besides, I'm not important enough in the firm to get this much attention, no matter what I did.* My heart was racing. Was the gig up? Was the joke on me? Was I going to be told they felt they'd made a mistake in extending me a job offer? What the hell was about to happen?

"Eric," Bob Segal said slowly, with the utmost professionalism, "I know you're going to Tampa tomorrow to take the bar exam, but we need to inform you that we're closing the West Palm Beach office." No one made a peep or looked at me. "We know this isn't what you wanted to hear."

Though I was instantly relieved I hadn't screwed up, I was completely confused.

"Your new boss, Howard Shapiro, and his colleague Howard Bregman have decided to start their own firm." He paused and watched my expression. I must have looked like I was handling the news okay, so he continued. "Not only is there no one to run the West Palm Beach branch, but Howard and his new partner are the big rainmakers in town. And if they take all the business, we don't have a reason to keep this office open. Understood?"

I nodded without speaking, wondering what was going to happen to me.

"Eric, you are welcome to come back to the Philadelphia office and join us there." At that point, several of the attorneys must have given themselves permission to make eye contact, as they did so with obligatory smiles. "Go ahead and take the bar exam tomorrow, think about it, and let us know."

A bunch of contradictory emotions were swirling around in my head as I left the office, but at least I wasn't fired. I didn't really have time to process the news before driving to Tampa the next day to take the exam. It was still important for me to pass. The day after returning from Tampa, Howard Shapiro and Howard Bregman had me over to their new offices and made me an offer.

"We want to bring you in, Eric, but we can only pay you $35,000 a year."

I'd still have my dream job, I thought, *but not the dream money*. Even so, Renée and I were having a great time in Florida, and it would be cool to get in on the ground floor of what was likely to be a very successful firm. I also knew I'd love working with athletes, to whom I could relate. I'd never feel out of place in this position. It was a great fit for my unique life experience as an aspiring lawyer. I thanked them both and told them I'd need a couple of days to think through everything.

Renée told me she'd support me no matter what my decision was, so I called my dad to get his take. He didn't mince words.

"Eric, you're making $62,500 in your current job and they're offering you only $35,000?" His sarcasm was not subtle. "Do the math and get your tush back up to Philly!" For my dad, money meant life security.

So that's what we did. Renée and I packed up and drove north. It was almost the exact trip I'd made when I'd driven down to Florida for college so many years earlier—only in the opposite direction.

I learned later that summer that I'd passed the Florida bar exam, so I was finally a legitimate lawyer, just in the wrong state. Upon arriving in Philadelphia and settling in, I had to start studying for the Pennsylvania bar exam. It was July, and I'd have to be ready for the exam by January, so for my first days at Wolf Block headquarters, they let me do low-level clerk stuff like writing memos and legal briefs and doing legal research so I could study. Everyone kind of left me on my own to cram because there wasn't much time to learn Pennsylvania law.

It was 1988, and Wolf Block was celebrating its one-hundred-year anniversary, so Renée and I were invited to the company's black-tie gala. Even though it was now March—well after I'd taken and passed the Pennsylvania bar and was now a qualified lawyer in *two* states—I was just starting my associate tasks and still hadn't gotten to know many of my colleagues. They had almost a full-year head start on me and were doing much more advanced legal work. I realized that the Florida office closing and my transfer back to the Philly office had really set me back. I chalked this up to everyone being so busy at such a prestigious law firm and me being the new guy on the block who was brought in hastily after the surprising turn of events in Florida. I remained optimistic that things would improve soon and that I'd find my role at headquarters.

Renée and I were looking forward to the gala so we could get dressed up for a night on the town, socialize with everyone at the firm, and hopefully meet some nice people and spark some new relationships. I especially wanted this for Renée, as she was so far from everything she'd known her whole life. From the culture to the climate to the pace and the landscape, Philly was completely different than Greenwood, South Carolina. Renée looked radiant as we left for the gala. She was wearing a black-and-gold gown, and I knew she would steal the show.

As we pulled up to the famed Union League of Philadelphia for the gala, I had a familiar feeling wash over me—a feeling I didn't belong. It reminded me of my first day at the prestigious Chestnut Hill Academy and my first day at USC law school when I felt I wasn't worthy. I wanted to call my father and brothers and tell them, "Can you believe I am about to go to a gala at the Union League?" No Bland had ever set foot in this exclusive venue. Sure, it hadn't ended well back at Chestnut Hill, but I'd made a lot of friends even though I didn't have as much money or come from the same social circles. I just hadn't been mature enough to settle down and do the work. This wasn't the case anymore. I could outwork anyone. I was a completely different person now—accomplished, confident, responsible, mature, and successful. I wouldn't screw up at Wolf Block; I'd dominate it. I just needed time. Still, the ghosts of my past were always present, and they were messing with my head big-time that night.

I wore a tux, and Renée looked gorgeous. I was so happy and proud to be entering this room of influential people with this radiant, confident woman on my arm. The love of my life would be at my side, and everything would be wonderful. She has always brought me strength and a sense of calm. As we entered the gala, I was leaning on her powers and fighting back my insecurities. With its private, who's-who membership, the Union League was built in the late 1800s with only the best materials. It is home to tons of mahogany, plenty of leather, and thick, dark carpets. The air was rich with the scent of bourbon, cognac, and only the most expensive cigars. To say the place was intimidating would be an understatement. For decades, Jews and minorities had not been allowed to be members or even enter its fashionable halls. It was a restricted venue.

We started making the rounds and meeting people. No surprise, but *everyone*—and I mean *everyone*—had graduated from an Ivy League law school. The guests at this event were law's cream of the crop. Princeton. University of Virginia. Yale. Harvard. Brown. Dartmouth. Name a top ten law school, and they were represented in the room. And there I was with degrees from the University of Tampa and University of South Carolina, both decent schools but without the prestige or reputation of an Ivy. I was talking with someone and noticed two senior lawyers talking to Renée a few feet away. They were clearly trying to impress her and couldn't get over her Southern accent. I walked over to introduce myself.

"Hello, I'm Eric Bland. Nice to meet you. I'm the new first-year hire."

They were polite but clearly disappointed that I'd interrupted their interaction with Renée. They asked what department I was in.

"Well, I'm going to be in litigation, but I'm still getting settled in. I was down at the West Palm Beach office and was transferred up here after they closed it."

They recalled the situation and shook their heads. "Oh, yeah, what a mess," the first guy said, patting me on the shoulder. "That must be why we don't remember recruiting you."

I smiled and nodded.

"So, where did you go to law school, Eric?"

"University of South Carolina."

I kid you not, at that, there was dead silence. Then, the first guy turned to the second, and right in front of my wife and me, as if we were ghosts, he said, "Wow, I didn't realize we recruited from schools like *that.*" They exchanged a few niceties after their insult and then made their way to the bar.

Right then and there, I knew I was screwed. I was just a warm body that Wolf Block had hired out of a sense of duty. They'd never promote me to become a partner. The partners had brought me to Philly because they felt bad about closing the West Palm Beach office after they'd extended an offer to me. They probably didn't want to get sued or have other recruits hear that they'd kicked a new hire to the curb. It was a sympathy offer to cover their asses, not an invite based on my skills, personality, hard work, or merit. It didn't matter that I'd passed the Pennsylvania *and* Florida bar exams on my first try. It didn't matter that I was capable of great legal work. It didn't matter that I was in the top 10 percent of my class because it wasn't the "right" school. None of it mattered because I didn't have the pedigree or connections. Just like the pool party when I was a clerk, this exchange left me reeling. But this time, it wasn't just tattoos I'd have to remove; it was my whole education and background—not possible.

I'd let two legal pricks from Wolf Block tell me that I didn't belong and, in an instant, wipe away what little self-confidence I had developed as a result of my academic success in college and law school. It was all gone with a single blow. When I look back on that moment today, I don't feel sorry for myself; I cringe. I had such an inferiority complex. I never thought I was worthy. I never thought I belonged. Back then, I still yearned to be accepted. These days, I won't let anyone take away or destroy my self-esteem and confidence. I don't care about belonging. I'm fine being an outsider. In fact, it has a lot of advantages. Today, the only thing that matters to me is being *respected*. There's a big difference between being accepted and respected. I didn't understand that back then. Now, I do. Today, I'm fierce because that's what the legal profession and the pursuit of justice demand. Yes, some days I'm still my own worst enemy, but I have learned to harness my fears and doubts. I'd come a long way on my personal journey by 1988, but I still had so much more work to do. In the end, those two lawyers did me a favor. They caused me to double down in my work and silence the noise around me. Once again, I would turn a snide remark into rocket fuel. I became hyperfocused on success. Today, those two lawyers at the Wolf Block gala couldn't hold a jockstrap to my achievements in the legal profession. Thanks, guys!

CHAPTER 7

MOVING ON

"There is a higher court than courts of justice and that is the court of conscience. It supersedes all other courts."

—*Mahatma Gandhi*

My plan was always to have my own business. When I became a lawyer, I often thought about how I could have my own law practice someday. As a kid watching my dad deal with his abusive boss, long commute, and eventual firing, I'd vowed to become the master of my own universe. That's what business ownership meant to me. I was never going to allow my destiny to be shaped by someone else. But at the time, I was too green and too poor to go out on my own. I needed the $67,500 second-year salary Wolf Block was paying me, and I needed to acquire professional skills and experience—to practice law in the real world. So, just as I had in college and law school, I put my nose to the grindstone.

New lawyers at Wolf Block were required to work eight months in three different departments—litigation, corporate, and labor—before being permanently placed. The hours were brutal. Even though I could outwork anyone, I was working next to people who were at the top of their game. They were smarter than me, could write better than me, and were lightning fast at legal research. Most were scholars who'd written for their university's law reviews, where they'd received incredible training on how to construct legal cases, defend cases, and write briefs. And they all had pedigree. I felt out of my league every day. Amid all the stress, you were required to reach a minimum billing requirement of two thousand hours per year. Since you can't bill for everything—hey, a guy's gotta eat—the pressure to work long hours to meet that billing requirement was intense. I was working fourteen hours a day and on weekends too. The firm published everyone's billed hours on a monthly basis, encouraging competition, embarrassment, and bragging.

Renée was amazing through it all. Here was this lovely, intelligent woman from rural South Carolina whom I'd whisked off to a major Northeastern city where she knew no one. But instead of pouting that she never got to see her new husband, she started working in the accounting department at John Wanamaker, an upscale clothing store located in downtown Philly. At the time, we were living near the City Line Avenue R5 Paoli local train stop, which was the last stop before the 30th Street Station near the University of Pennsylvania campus, where I would disembark and start the long-ass walk to my office on 20th and Market Street. Each morning, train after train would pass me by because they were filled to the gills with people from all the previous stops—Malvern, Villanova, Ardmore, Lancaster, and many more. By the time the train got to me, there wasn't a seat left, so I'd have to wait and wait and wait.

The ride home was also long and exhausting, especially on a Friday after a hard week. At 4:45 p.m. on Friday afternoons, I'd be cramming in some last-minute research in the law library when a senior partner would walk in and motion for me to come to the door.

"Hey, Eric," they'd whisper. "Come here. I've got a little memo I need you to write for me this weekend. It won't take much time, but I need it by Monday morning."

It seemed to happen every Friday in the library, or even on the elevator when I was leaving the office. All the new lawyers like me worked on the twenty-seventh or twenty-eighth floor. There was a stop at an elevator bank on the twelfth floor, which was also the partners' floor. You'd have to get off and change elevators there, and every Friday, as you either rushed to your desk in the morning or hurried out of the building to catch your train in the evening, you'd hit that elevator bank, the doors would open, and there would be a senior partner waiting for you with a "little" assignment that "wouldn't take too much time." This "little" project usually ended up ruining your weekend. Not only did it take much longer than the partner said it would, but you would spend the entire weekend scared shitless that you'd gotten it wrong because you were doing this little memo for a brilliant senior partner who basically held your future in the palm of their hands. To make things worse, on Monday, they would hit you with the joke's punch line. First thing, you'd rush into the partner's office and tell your boss's secretary that the little memo they wanted was ready. You'd hand it off and try to catch your breath as the secretary looked over the top of a set of horn-rimmed reading glasses with no small sense of annoyance and tell you that the partner in question would not be back until Wednesday.

In your head, you were screaming, *What the fuck?!* But in front of the secretary, you would simply nod, smile politely, and say, "Thank you," with just the slightest hint of sarcasm. Yes, this was the eighties, and these moments were much like the famous *Animal House* scene where Kevin Bacon screamed, "Thank you, sir, may I have another?" as he was paddled during his fraternity initiation. After a few weeks, I was wise to what was basically a hazing ritual, a twisted exercise to beat down the newbies. Maybe the partners at Wolf Block saw it as some sort of rite of passage.

But once I got wise, I was having none of it. There was no way I was going to keep playing a game I had no chance of winning. So, every Friday, I would skip the elevators and *walk* up and down all twenty-eight floors just to avoid the "little memo" trap that awaited me on the twelfth-floor elevator bank or in the library. I'm not going to lie, it was a lot of stairs, but it was worth it just to save my sanity and get my weekends back so Renée and I could enjoy one of the best small/big cities in America.

In the end, I got the last laugh. One Friday afternoon, having sprinted down all those stairs, I was walking to the train in a particularly good mood when I heard my name.

I turned around and saw my old friend Lee Rosengard. "Lee?"

"Eric," he grabbed me in a big friendly bear hug, "What the hell are you doing here?"

"I work at Wolf Block right around the corner," I explained.

When I was interviewing for jobs in the fall of my third year of law school, I'd interviewed with Lee, who was the hiring partner at the prestigious law firm of Stradley, Ronon, Stevens & Young. I had received a job offer from that firm after graduation from law school but hadn't accepted it. I actually liked Lee the best of all of the hiring partners I'd interviewed with, but Wolf Block offered me the most money. Foolishly, I'd chosen my first job in law based on money alone.

"I thought you were supposed to be in West Palm Beach, Florida, not Philly," Lee said, confused. "What happened?"

"Ha! Yeah, that's a long story," I laughed. "In a nutshell, they closed the West Palm Beach office, and I got transferred up here. I had to pass the bars in Florida *and* in Pennsylvania. It was a lot of studying, but it all worked out. Man, it's great to see you, Lee. So, what are you up to these days?"

The conversation flowed as we caught up, and Lee shared stories about his family and his practice. He was an attorney who wore a bow tie and had a very highbrow drawl, but deep down, he was just a hardworking guy from a modest background. His wife, Andrea, was also a lawyer and general counsel for ACME supermarkets, a well-known grocery store chain in Philadelphia.

"Eric, do you have a few minutes to come to my office Monday at lunch? I'd like you to meet some people."

Within a week, I had an offer to be a litigator at Stradley, but Lee couldn't quite match my Wolf Block salary. I was really looking for a raise to make the jump from the city's top firm, so I was torn. Sensing my hesitancy, Lee asked me to pop over at lunch.

"Eric, you like me, and I like you. I wanted you to come work for me from the start. You know that. So, let me be honest. You're not cut out for Wolf Block. I know it, and you know it. You're not Ivy League like most of their lawyers. That's going to hold you back there."

He was touching on one of my deepest concerns. From the start, I'd felt like an outsider, both socially and in the types of assignments I was receiving. Lee was Jewish like me, but his team was a mix of Ivy Leaguers and lawyers of all backgrounds, faiths, and law schools. It seemed like they hired the person, not the school. The firm had many Catholic lawyers who'd graduated from Villanova and Catholic University law schools because its largest client was the Archdiocese of Philadelphia. This was a big deal because the Archdiocese was the largest private landholder in Philadelphia, owning more than 15 percent of the land at that time.

"You're coming to work for me, Eric, okay? I'll get close to matching what you're making at Wolf Block."

That night, when I talked things over with Renée, she said, "Do it, Eric!" It felt really good to be wanted. The next day, I handed in my resignation and made the jump to Stradley, Ronon, Stevens & Young. Lee was right, I did get a lot more hands-on experience with big corporate law and litigation, and in the beginning, it did seem like a better fit. For one thing, I was in awe of attorney Bill Sasso, the firm's rainmaker. Not only was he a great lawyer, but he was also charismatic and persuasive, and boy, could he bring in the clients—I'm talking big deals! I watched him schmooze people and make them feel important. If you went to lunch or dinner with Bill, you were definitely hiring Stradley, Ronon, Stevens & Young as your law firm by the end of the meal. It was amazing to behold. I studied Bill's behavior—we all did. He absolutely owned the room. We were all like, "How is he doing this?" There were so many lawyers in Philadelphia, and he was probably only forty-five years old at the time. He gave a talk to those of us who were just starting out, and somebody asked him how he got so much business.

"Well," Bill replied, "you've got to learn how to ask."

One of the young lawyers in the room chimed in, "I'm asking all the time, but nobody's hiring me. I don't know how you close so much business."

"The secret is how, when, and whom you ask," Bill responded. "You've got to know the right person to ask and tell them what you can do for them. You can't just shake someone's hand at a cocktail party and then ask them to give you some legal business. That's not how it works. You need to get to know them personally, ask questions, listen, and understand their interests, where they are vulnerable, and what pain points you can help them address. That's where the opportunities are. Get to know people and then ask once you understand these things. Make sense?"

Everyone nodded but still seemed confused.

"Let me tell you a story," Bill continued. "I haven't always been this successful at closing business. In fact, my first seven or eight years as a lawyer, I was just like you guys—always wondering where my next client would come from. It was stressful. Well, my wife and I had these really good friends, and the husband owned a big steel fabrication business. Despite traveling and going out together regularly for many years, he never gave me any business. So, one day, we were playing tennis, and I finally asked him. 'Look, we've been great friends for a long time. You know I work for a large law firm. You know I am a respected lawyer. How come you've never given me any business?' And you know what my good friend said? 'You never asked.'"

Bill Sasso's approach to landing business had a huge impact me and would influence the way I built relationships and did business later in my career when I was finally able to lead my own law firm. I am not afraid to ask for anything. What is the worst thing that can happen? You get a no. I will take ninety-nine nos for one yes. If you're afraid and not willing to lose, then you're not willing to win.

The first big case I worked on at Stradley was a medical malpractice case. It involved a young woman whose breast reduction surgery had gone terribly wrong. My boss, Lee, was the lead lawyer on the case. I enjoyed the preparation for the trial. The medical team had measured the woman's breasts while she was leaning back on a tilted table instead of standing up. This was a huge mistake. Breast reduction patients should always be measured standing up so that when they reconstruct the breast after the reduction, everything gets put back where it naturally belongs. It's just common sense when you think about it. But since this was not the case, the medical team's measurements were off—and I mean way off. When they went to replace her areola after the surgical procedure to remove tissue to reduce the size of the woman's breasts, the doctor placed her areolas closer to her clavicle than her breasts. The measurement was off by two or three inches. The error was so egregious, any layperson could look at a single photo of this woman post-surgery and know that the doctor and his team had undeniably made a horrific mistake.

In addition to profound physical disfigurement, the young woman, who was only in her twenties, had suffered significant anxiety and embarrassment after the surgery. Obviously, she would have to go through subsequent surgeries to rectify the mistake, and this would cause substantial scarring. It seemed like the case would settle because the mistake was so glaring—but that was not the case. The surgeon thought the jury would exonerate him. He was an arrogant man. In our law office, he was referred to as "Dr. Tilt" for how he measured our client's breasts before the surgery. He and his legal team wanted a trial. Big mistake. The jury returned a verdict for more than $5 million, which in 1980s dollars was a large verdict. It was the right result. This taught me that you only go to trial with good cases. Don't think you're so good that you can turn a chickenshit case into chicken salad.

For me, this case cemented the fact that I wanted to represent victims, people who had been wronged, as this woman had. I wanted justice for her. It disturbed me to see how things were sometimes handled by other lawyers. This reinforced my desire to have my own law firm. I wanted to practice law the way I wanted to practice law—in the best interest of my clients. These types of cases were career catalysts, pivotal moments that shaped my thinking about wanting to be independent as quickly as possible. In the breast reduction case, at least, I felt I was on the right side, which was important to me. This would not always be the case.

As I mentioned, one of the biggest clients my colleagues Bill Sasso and senior litigation partner Jack O'Dea managed at Stradley Ronon was the Archdiocese of Philadelphia. We handled all their legal needs—everything from slips and falls in a church community room during bingo to property transactions to priest or nun issues to a child getting hurt on the playground at a Catholic school. They were a huge client and, for a time, made up more than 50 percent of my caseload. Some of the cases alleged that certain priests were sexually abusing nuns or other females. As one would expect, the Archdiocese, which encompassed more than two hundred parishes, aggressively defended these cases. But it seemed to me that the law firm's senior partners were working very closely with church's hierarchy. After a while, the whole thing started to get to me. These were special cases. Only the top litigators would work on these matters. Young associates like me were not assigned to these files. Even early in my career, I understood that a lawyer's job was to problem solve and not to judge. And not every case I saw brought against the clergy or the church in Philly had merit. But what I saw in the cases that did appear to have merit seemed to perpetuate a horrific problem where young people were caught in the middle. People's lives were being destroyed, and no one seemed to be doing anything to stop it. Money awards or settlements cannot cure every problem. Some matters cause so much psychological trauma that money just cannot solve them. From where I sat, it seemed like the church and priests were sometimes being protected more than the victimized parishioners, nuns, females, or youths. Personally, I felt like I was on the wrong side of these cases, and I didn't like that feeling at all. I wanted to scream. These were men of the cloth who were breaking their vows to God and preying on the vulnerable and weak. I was old enough to understand that the Catholic church did not have a monopoly on this type of problem. Religious leaders from other faiths have also abused their positions, but this was my first and only experience with these types of cases. To further compound the problem, the world later learned that the senior officials in the church would sometimes make the victims and their families feel guilty for continuing with their claims against the church. It was horrifying to witness, and yet another powerful experience that fueled my desire to go out on my own and represent victims.

The other reality that was becoming abundantly clear to me was that bringing in new business in Philly was damned hard. There was so much pressure to bill hours and bring in new clients, but it seemed like every person in Philly already had a "good" lawyer. Either they had grown up with a friend who'd become a lawyer, had run a business together, or had attended the same school or church. It was nearly impossible to find someone without a lawyer. This was becoming a big problem. I'd once had a very strong network in Philly, but having been gone for so long, it had dissolved, which put me at a disadvantage. I'd kept in touch with Joe Connell—yep, the Mormon with six kids who was my best friend from law school—and we spoke regularly. He'd finally left a large law firm in Camden, South Carolina, to start his own personal injury firm and was doing well.

"You know, Eric, the business law you practice and the type of law you want to do, well, nobody does that down here. Everybody is either doing car wrecks or medical malpractice, but business lawyers are rare here."

Though I couldn't imagine leaving Philly at the time, Joe's observation made me think. I kept circling back to his observation, especially on days when I was struggling to meet my annual two thousand billable hours quota, which was often. I continued to learn how to be a strong litigator at Stradley Ronan over the course of the next year. The next big case I worked on involved Texaco, the giant gasoline distributor. Texaco was in a dispute with one of its franchisees. The lawyer on the opposing side of the case was Steven Kapustin from a suburban Philly firm called Boroff, Harris & Heller in Plymouth Meeting, just outside the city and about a mile from where I'd grown up. Steven was a tough Jewish lawyer—very streetwise—and I respected him. He was a formidable opponent.

After the case wrapped up, he took me out to lunch and said, "You realize you're never going get the legal skills you need working at a big firm like Stradley, Ronon, Stevens & Young, right? It's not going to happen for at least eight more years. Until then, you'll just be second or third chair on every case. That's the reality at these big firms. You'll argue motions in court and take a few depositions, but you certainly won't get first-chair trial experience."

I shrugged but kept listening. I was learning and getting more experience on some of the big cases I was part of at Stradley Ronon. But deep down, I knew Steven was right. I wasn't in charge of any cases; I was just supporting other lawyers from the bench.

"I like you, Eric. I like how you talk. You look people in the eye. You're confident. I want you to come work for me. I'll pay you close to what you're getting paid at Stradley because I need a guy like you."

At this point in my legal career, gaining experience was now more important than a bigger salary. So, in pursuit of bigger challenges, I made yet another jump and joined Boroff, Harris & Heller to work with Steven and his team. I wanted to handle a case from start to finish on my own, and this seemed like the right opportunity. Even after this move, there was a voice in my head reminding me about how I didn't like the way corporate law was practiced in Philly and about Joe's comments that South Carolina needed more business lawyers. In general, though, life was good. Renée and I were happy and enjoying every minute of our time together. In fact, after the initial culture shock, Renée had settled into Philly and was loving city life—more than I was, actually. After Wanamaker's, she was offered a new job with The Gap as a store manager. Retail has long, long hours. We'd rented a row house in a quaint town called Gladwyne, and Renée caught a nice break. She started working with the Philadelphia Suburban Water Company in their internal accounting office. Renée was content. But much to my surprise, I was missing South Carolina's beautiful weather and still dreaming of my own law practice, which would be next to impossible to start in Philly's competitive landscape. Then, as fortune would have it, South Carolina came back into my life through the back door, just like an old friend. I'd say back porch door, but we don't really have those in Philly.

CHAPTER 8

MOVING SOUTH

"Expect the unexpected. And whenever possible BE the unexpected. Always be ready."

—*Lynda Barry*

It was sort of a crazy coincidence how Renée and I ended up moving back to South Carolina. At the time, a suburban Philadelphia law firm named Boroff, Harris & Heller was representing a businessman named Ken Hyatt, who owned the largest Chrysler Plymouth dealership in Columbia, South Carolina. What were the odds? Ken Hyatt's reputation for getting sued was so widespread, he couldn't get a lawyer to represent him in his home state. A Charleston malpractice lawyer named Ellis Kahn told Hyatt that he had a friend in Philly who was a hell of a business litigator, and his name was Steven Kapustin. That's right, my new boss. So, that's how Ken Hyatt from Columbia, South Carolina, hired Boroff, Harris & Heller in Philadelphia to represent him.

Hyatt was a huge man with a big beard. His TV commercials were on everywhere in Columbia. He'd walk up and down the big rows of cars on his huge lot and say, "Come on over to

Ken Hyatt Chrysler Plymouth for an unbeatable deal. I'll sell you a car for only one dollar over invoice." This slogan, as you can imagine, was very popular. Hyatt sold a lot of cars this way. But the people who bought the cars couldn't always afford them. So, the Chrysler Corporation was suing Hyatt to recover losses on the financing side, because many loans had defaulted and too many cars had been repossessed. Hyatt was responsible for the shortfall based on recourse financing—and it was alleged that he was not paying because he contended that Chrysler Capital had breached their obligations to him. Since I was Steven Kapustin's new right-hand man at the law firm, I started working on Ken's largest files and having some success. We were working closely to get everything settled with Chrysler to the point that Ken stopped calling Steven and just started reaching out to me directly. I was enjoying the experience of working with a major client so directly and traveling back and forth to South Carolina. It finally felt like I was getting to practice corporate law in the big leagues.

On one of my trips to Columbia, Ken said to me, "If you come back to South Carolina, I'll give you all my legal work. You can set up your own firm, and I'll be your first big client." In addition to his automobile dealerships, Ken owned several other major ancillary businesses and two very successful miniature golf courses in Myrtle Beach, South Carolina.

"Why do I want to keep working with Boroff, Harris & Heller, Eric? I want someone local. I want to work with you, not them."

The opportunity to open my own practice had landed right in my lap, and oddly enough, it was in Columbia, South Carolina.

I told Renée what I wanted to do. She was surprised I wanted to leave Philly, but as always, she was supportive.

I told my dad, who said I'd be crazy to leave such a lucrative job and big paycheck. "Eric, how can a Jewish boy from Philly grow a successful law practice in Columbia, South Carolina?"

I knew it was risky, but my intuition was telling me to bet on myself, which was exactly what I decided to do. I was thirty years old, and I was finally going to open my own law firm. Secretly, I took the South Carolina bar exam and decided to tell my boss, Steven, about my plan, months before getting the results. I was hoping he'd be supportive, but I also realized I'd be taking a big client away from his firm. Our conversation could go either way. Steven was mad but said I could take Ken Hyatt as a client—with one stipulation. He wanted me to leave immediately. This was not the plot twist I'd expected, but I respected my boss's position and cleared out my office the same day. It was a good lesson. I now advise my clients as follows: if an employee quits or you fire them, ask them to leave immediately. Nothing good happens if you let them work after notice has been given. They might create chaos, download files, or contact your customers or vendors. Don't open your company up to these sorts of risks.

It was late July of 1991, and I wasn't going to know if I'd passed the South Carolina bar exam until the end of October—almost three months away, which was an eternity in my mind. With everything on the line, Renée and I packed up our row house in Philly and headed to her parents' second home on Lake Murray, just outside of Columbia. It was the first time we'd ever lived in a single-family home, and I remember immediately liking the feeling. I was so grateful that her parents let us live in the house rent-free, and they even signed for a credit line for me with County Bank so I would have the money to open my law practice. Even before taking the bar exam, I'd already reached out to my law school friend Joe Connell. We'd agreed that if I ever moved back, we'd work together. As soon as I received news that I'd passed the bar, we opened our practice, Connell & Bland. We really weren't law partners, just associates. It was a true eat-what-you-kill arrangement, except when we worked together on a case.

Ken Hyatt kept me plenty busy that first year with his dealerships and other businesses, and I was so grateful. But Joe and I were also starting to litigate—and win—other cases against some big-name lawyers in the area. What was interesting was that some of my opponents' clients were not happy with their representation and wanted to work with me after watching me in the courtroom and observing my litigation skills, and this became a huge growth driver over time. Business was picking up, and it didn't take long for me to start making as much money as I had in Philly. From that point on, my income and reputation as a lawyer kept growing nicely every year. I liked working with Joe and having my own firm. Connell & Bland was thriving, and as our network grew, Joe introduced me to a well-connected man named Tom Milliken, who was the campaign manager for longtime South Carolina senator Ernest "Fritz" Hollings, the esteemed conservative Democrat who, at the time, was defending his seat in the United States Senate, where he'd been representing South Carolina since 1966. So, not only was our network growing, but it was also becoming more influential. In 1992, presidential candidate Bill Clinton spoke at our law offices in Camden, South Carolina, during his successful campaign to unseat Republican incumbent President George H. W. Bush. It was exciting to be part of it. We were making a name for ourselves. After working together on a few cases, Tom asked Joe and I to join his firm. For a short time, we were Milliken, Connell, & Bland. Renée and I moved from Lake Murray to an antebellum mansion in Camden, and life was good.

Along the way, Tom also introduced me to one of the most important connections of my career, John Ducate, founder of Ducane Gas Grills, which was one of the largest companies in South Carolina at the time. In the winter, the company ran a monster furnace business, and in the summer, they sold high-end gas barbecue grills. Originally from New Jersey, John was a big, tough Italian guy, and we immediately clicked. He referred to me as his "Philadelphia lawyer," his "bulldog." It wasn't long before he treated me like a son and took it upon himself to find me new business. The first case he brought me on involved his daughter Nina who was seventeen years old at the time. Nina's so-called friends had gone joyriding on the Ducate's street after she had broken up with her boyfriend. One of them had fired a bullet through one of the home's windows to send a signal to Nina. John was livid and decided to send a signal right back. He wanted us to take the group's parents to court for negligent supervision and negligent entrustment of an automobile to a minor. I ended up getting enough money from the settlement to pay for Nina's college at Clemson University, and then some.

John Ducate knew I was the real deal, so recalling the sales wisdom of attorney Bill Sasso from Philly, I asked John to give me some of his corporate business, which had all been with well-regarded attorney Terry Richardson at South Carolina's Motley Rice, one of the world's largest and most successful law firms. Motley Rice was the firm behind some of America's biggest asbestos and tobacco class action suits. Ron Motley and Joe Rice enjoyed international reputations as major litigators. They settled cases against gigantic conglomerates in the hundreds of millions of dollars. At first, John was hesitant but said he did have one piece of litigation in Florida, where a distributor had gone bankrupt and stuck him with a receivable for $800,000 worth of grills that had not been paid for.

"I'll give you that business if you can show me where to get that money, Eric," John told me.

Remember, I had a Florida lawyer's license from my short time in West Palm Beach, so I dug in and uncovered some surprising information. Apparently, the distributor was in financial trouble and was buying the grills from Ducane on credit, then selling them to Ace Hardware Stores and other retailers in an attempt to pay off its bank loan and stay afloat. The bank knew the distributor was slowly going bankrupt and started ratcheting down its line of credit. But over a two-year period, when Ducane's CFO Ira Zolin would have conversations with the bank and ask how business was going for the distributor, the bank administrators would say, "Fine." They didn't want to get stung on the loan and needed Ducane Grills to keep providing gas grills to the distributor on credit so the distributor could keep producing revenue to pay off the bank loan. The bank administrators were hiding all this. When the distributor finally went under, Ducane Grills was left with a big unpaid bill. On behalf of the company, I sued the bank in Florida State Court. We achieved an excellent settlement, recovering six figures. Over the course of the next couple of years, John Ducate started moving a significant portion of Ducane's legal business from Motley Rice over to me. I owe so much to John. Not only did he help me start my firm and build a reputation as a strong litigator, but he also pushed me over the years to cement that reputation. Everyone needs a champion in their lives, and John was mine. He bragged about me to his friends, business associate, and fellow CEOs. He took it upon himself to get me more clients, for which I am forever grateful.

Another big client early in my South Carolina days was Don Galloway Homes out of Charlotte, North Carolina. The company paid a lawyer to handle their real estate and land closings in Charleston, South Carolina. As part of each home closing, the buyer had to have title insurance. But the Charleston lawyer was charging Don Galloway Homes construction title insurance premiums instead of permanent home premium rates. In other words, the Charleston lawyer was overcharging for the wrong type of title insurance—by a lot. The problem had been going on for about five years to the tune of about $100,000 in overcharges, which was big money in 1994. It was a legal malpractice case, which you almost never heard of back in the day. Lawyers just didn't sue other lawyers. In fact, Don Galloway couldn't find a lawyer willing to sue a fellow lawyer. The lawyer on the other side of the case was a good defense lawyer and was kind to me. We became friendly, and I bet one dollar that I would get my client most of his money back. He took the bet. I won. True to his word, he paid up at the conclusion of the case. I framed the dollar, which still hangs on the office wall today. After I won the case, Don Galloway Homes gave me most of their significant legal work in North and South Carolina. For the remainder of the nineties, this book of business represented about 60 percent of my revenue.

I always found Don Galloway's predicament interesting. How was it that he couldn't find a lawyer to sue another lawyer? Lawyers don't have any trouble suing other professionals, like engineers, doctors, and architects. Why should lawyers be exempt from legal scrutiny? They put their pants on one leg at a time just like everyone else. But in the state of South Carolina, lawyers seemed to be exempt from legal scrutiny. In fact, at the time, there was only one lawyer in the whole state taking on legal malpractice suits—one lawyer! How could that be?

Lawyers don't work in silos like professionals in many other industries. For the most part, they all know one another because they find themselves thrown together in courtrooms— often on opposite sides of cases. A lawyer might go up against the same law firm in multiple cases and get to know all the lawyers on their team. Through these encounters, lawyers and the firms they work for build reputations in certain industry segments. For example, there are lawyers and law firms that handle product liability or medical malpractice cases, as well as those who handle political matters and lobbying issues. You learn a lot about lawyers and law firms in a courtroom. Did they do a good job for their client? Did they do their homework or miss key points? Were they prepared, timely, and professional? Were they eloquent in their written and verbal communications? Did they play fair or dirty? Did they sell their client short? So, even when you're working against one another, you start to learn which lawyers you respect and which you don't.

Outside of work, lawyers tend to run in the same social groups. They play golf at the same country clubs, go to the same churches, send their kids to the same private schools, and support the same nonprofits. In short, lawyers stick together. They're all networking in their communities to build relationships and their businesses. Additionally, when firms have case requests they can't handle, they refer clients to other firms they trust. For all these reasons, lawyers form close-knit communities and networks. In these communities, there are often unspoken agreements about having one another's back. Right or wrong, there's a code of protection—lawyers don't sue other lawyers. Unfortunately, this means that a lot of negligent and bad legal behavior isn't scrutinized and goes unredressed. There's no accountability. Often, clients are unaware that their lawyers have made mistakes and sometimes even covered up those mistakes. Who loses in these situations? Clients who have been wronged by their lawyers. This doesn't sit well with me. Bad behavior is bad behavior. I'm a very client-driven lawyer. If a client shows me that a lawyer or law firm has wronged them, I'm going after those lawyers. I am not deterred by my profession's code of protection. The cases belong to the clients, not the lawyers. But back in the eighties and nineties, that wasn't how it worked in South Carolina. In taking on the Don Galloway Homes case against a lawyer, I'd crossed some kind of invisible line that shielded lawyers from scrutiny—no matter how bad their behavior. Some of what I would see in the coming years was really, really bad—and I'm not even talking about Alex Murdaugh's crimes yet. My first step over this line with Don Galloway Homes didn't make too many waves. But in the not-too-distant future, suing other lawyers would change the trajectory of my life forever.

Attorney Dick Harpootlian, who is now widely known as a South Carolina senator as well as for his role as the lead defender in the Alex Murdaugh trial, wasn't quite so famous when I was first introduced to him in the mid-1990s. Around 1994, Harpootlian had decided to stop being a solicitor for the

Fifth Judicial Circuit in Richland County, South Carolina, and entered into private law practice. We were introduced, and he began referring me some video poker and personal injury cases. Soon, I was representing some of the biggest video poker clients in South Carolina, companies like Collins Entertainment, Great Games of North Augusta, and Rock Hill Amusement Company. These were the companies that had developed and were distributing a machine called the "Pot of Gold" because it made so much money. The companies would place these machines in convenience stores and video-poker parlors on the borders of North Carolina and Georgia, states where video poker was prohibited, so the citizens of these states would cross state lines and come to play the machines. It was big money.

I started getting a reputation as a video poker lawyer. It was a highly lucrative business. Locations and routes were extremely competitive. Different companies would pay to place their machines over a competitor's machines in an establishment. There was intense litigation around this in the nineties. The industry was also controversial because people were getting hooked and betting their livelihoods playing these games. As politicians started to push back on the industry, I represented the people who built the machines, arguing they were games of skill, not games of chance. This slight variation in definition meant the difference between being regulated as video games versus gambling machines. It was a make-or-break difference for these companies, because being defined as gambling machines was likely to kill the industry altogether. In the end, after years of running booming businesses in the area, legislators defined them as gambling machines and a major crackdown began. The entire industry—and the strong legal business I'd built around it—was brought to a complete halt.

Around the same time, in 1996, Joe Connell and I had decided to separate our law practices. Joe was doing mainly real-estate closings and personal-injury cases that would settle before trial. My practice had grown around complex commercial and catastrophic injury cases, many of which would not settle and had to be litigated and tried. We separated on good terms and have remained close to this day. In fact, Joe's son Ben, who is a well-known lawyer and legislator in the South Carolina House of Representatives, is like a godson to me. Ben is one of the most amazing men I have ever met. He was the high school national heavyweight champion his senior year and the best high school wrestler South Carolina has ever produced. He is huge and strong. We work cases together now. What sets him apart is that he is a righteous man, as well as a great father and husband. I love him and look up to him.

I'd gone independent in 1991 with the help of Ken Hyatt, my first big client, and my good friend Joe. Ever since, I'd been riding a nice long wave of financial stability and growth with a number of large, successful clients. But in a matter of two years, things changed dramatically. My video poker clients were gone due to changes in the law. I helped Don Galloway sell his company to a larger homebuilder in 1998. John Ducate had fallen on tough times and was also getting ready to sell Ducane's gas and oil furnace business, which was a big part of their business. As I looked ahead to the beginning of the new century, my prospects were a bit fuzzy. Basically, my hourly corporate business was drying up. I was staring into an abyss, and it was stressful. But, as has often been the case in my life, a big opportunity presented itself, and I grabbed it.

CHAPTER 9

LAWYER VERSUS LAWYER

"Keep your friends close; keep your enemies closer."

—*Sun Tzu*

A s I mentioned earlier, Dick Harpootlian had referred a lot of business to me in the nineties. We'd become close, and through him, I met many influential people in the state. I had been introduced to Dick by former family court judge and Republican state senator Larry Richter, who was running for attorney general in 1994. These powerful men all ran in the same circles and looked out for one another. At the time, there were numerous signals I missed around how these people operated. But I was young and eager, so I dismissed my concerns or made excuses for their behaviors. For instance, while I was working cases with Larry, he told me it would be "good for my career" if I bought Dick Harpootlian a computer for his new office. Dick was just opening his private practice and had no office equipment at the time. Being "encouraged" to make these purchases,

Renée and I went to Circuit City and bought Dick his first office computer and printer, which were not so ubiquitous back then and quite expensive. As the surprising events of the coming years would unfold, the memory of these purchases would become quite ironic to me.

Larry Richter also ran a successful Charleston-based law firm, where a talented young lawyer named Ronald L. Richter Jr. was holding down the fort while his boss and cousin attended to a growing list of political commitments. Ronnie, as he was called, was handling more and more of the firm's caseload, even though he was a young lawyer. We were meeting up in a lot of courtrooms, in meetings, and in depositions, and watching each other handle cases. We were also handling some cases together due to my affiliation with the Richter law firm. Though we had extremely different approaches and polar-opposite personalities, we quickly came to respect each other as lawyers and men. It didn't take me long to realize Ronnie was a very talented lawyer. He was a great writer with a cunning intellect. We really gelled as friends too. We talked sports. We were both golfers. Neither of us were born into privilege. We even loved some of the same shows and movies like *The Big Lebowski*, *Things to Do in Denver When You're Dead*, and basically anything created by the Coen brothers.

In 1997, we tried a medical malpractice case together in Chester County, South Carolina. It was a ruptured appendix case that could have been prevented if the doctors had not missed the diagnosis. The male patient suffered significant peritonitis in his abdominal area. The closing arguments were on February 26, 1997, a day I'll never forget because it was the day my son, Davis, was born. I had to leave immediately after the closing arguments to rush to the hospital to be with my family. The jury came back in the evening with a $250,000 verdict in favor of our client. We were told that, at the time, it was the largest jury verdict ever in Chester County. Ronnie and I knew from that day forward we had something special together. We were a good team—better together than separate.

Ronnie had been working with and for Larry Richter for about four years when he told his cousin he wanted to be made a partner. Larry said that was absolutely doable—with one hitch. To become a full partner at Richter Law Firm, Ronnie would have to go through a multiyear buy-in period. This meant that even though Ronnie was handling most of the daily grind on the larger cases for the firm, he was going to have to pay Larry over the course of several years until he'd paid off the purchase price. This was the only way Ronnie could become a full partner in the firm. This didn't make sense or seem fair to Ronnie.

"Larry, I'm pretty sure I could take the same amount of money I'd be paying you," Ronnie told his boss and cousin, "and hang my own shingle." After making the statement, Ronnie got up from the table, thanked Larry, left the meeting, and walked away from his job.

Even without iPhones and social media, this kind of news traveled fast in legal circles. Larry was spreading the word that he was going to make Ronnie regret leaving his firm. He told everyone that he expected Ronnie to come crawling back soon, begging for his old job. Larry considered Ronnie's departure a tremendous act of disloyalty, and so did Larry's lawyer friends. Not twenty-four hours later, I received a call came from Larry's close friend Dick Harpootlian.

"Eric," he said, skipping all the small talk to get straight to the point, "I know you are great friends with Ronnie, but he's got to feel the pain. Do not refer him any work. If you do, we will cut you off."

The threat could not have been clearer.

I wasn't even six years into having my own law practice, which these powerful and well-connected people had helped me build, and now they were telling me that if I didn't comply with this single "request," a good chunk of my business would be taken away and I'd no longer be welcome in the influential circles into which they'd invited me. I was sure other lawyers were getting a similar message, but I was the closest to Ronnie. Larry and his lawyer friends were trying to wield their power over everyone to get Ronnie to comply. *So, this is how the game is played*, I thought.

I remember going home to talk things over with Renée, who could see how distressed I was about the tremendous decision I had to make. I wanted to work with Ronnie more, not less. I respected him tremendously, and we were friends. *How could we be professionally cut off from each other?* I thought. *It's unthinkable! How could anybody treat him this way? He's such a talented lawyer, and he's my friend.* Then, of course, I talked things over with my ever ethical and loyal dad. I admired these rare and important qualities in my father and wanted to emulate him in this regard.

"What do you want to do, Eric?" my dad asked matter-of-factly. "What do you think is the right thing to do?"

"Dad, I don't know if it's that simple. I mean this is my livelihood. I could lose everything. But I have a great friend in Ronnie. He makes me a better lawyer, and I make him a better lawyer."

"Then I guess you've got your answer, son. And I promise you, it's simpler than you think. So, are you willing to feel the pain? It might last for two years or maybe even up to five years. But if Ronnie's that good, and if you guys are that good together, you'll overcome whatever Dick Harpootlian, Larry Richter, and their powerful lawyer friends throw at you."

As usual, my dad was right. When you do what's right, the answers to even life's most difficult questions and challenges are actually very straightforward. Of course, *simple* doesn't always mean *easy*. In fact, doing what's right typically isn't the easiest path, but it will get you to the right destination—and in the long run, that's what matters.

After the call with my dad, I decided to support my friend and do business with Ronnie no matter the consequences. Early in his career, he'd been involved with some big-time litigation cases, including the legal case against USAir after Flight 1016 crashed during landing in 1994 at the Charlotte/Douglas International Airport amid bad weather. But to break free from his cousin's law firm, he had to take on small stuff so he could make ends meet as he rebuilt his career. He started doing magistrate court stuff and family court law. That's how important it was for him to go independent. So, we were both running our own firms, but when there was a litigation case we could work on together, or one that warranted two attorneys, we shared it. That's how it all started: first with a single case, then a second, third, fourth, and so on. We were splitting things fifty-fifty and getting in a groove. A few years later, the Bland Richter law firm was born, and Ronnie and I have never looked back. But at the time, the future looked unclear. All my big hourly clients had dried up, and now Harpootlian and his lawyer friends were refusing to refer me any business. Income was down to a trickle.

Luckily, I got a call from a friend of mine, a horse guy from Camden. He asked me if I'd be interested in a legal malpractice case against one of the largest law firms in South Carolina, Nexsen Pruet. I told him I'd handled a legal malpractice case before, so yes, I was interested. He said his friend Jimmy Myrick was trying to buy and develop a tomato farm on a few hundred acres in Wadmalaw, South Carolina, but needed financing to finalize the deal and was facing a contractual deadline he might not be able to meet. Nexsen Pruet was representing Jimmy Myrick, but when they saw their client might not be able to meet the contractual deadline, it was alleged that they assisted a different client, a competitor, in buying the property from underneath his feet. That's right, they were allegedly picking winners and losers between their clients and screwing Jimmy Myrick, a paying client, in order to keep the deal alive. As the case developed, my law firm alleged that they helped their other client take advantage of the time gap created when the county denied Jimmy Myrick's development plan. Basically, this would make it possible for their other client to swoop in, buy the land, develop it, and make a fortune—while leaving Jimmy Myrick out in the cold. Ronnie and I couldn't believe it. Not only did we want this work to keep money coming into our firm, but we were both shocked by how wrong this behavior was, especially from such a large and supposedly reputable law firm. Lawyers can't do this kind of thing to their clients. It's a conflict of interest. Lawyers have a fiduciary responsibility to their clients. We were shocked.

In an attempt to explain their actions, Nexsen Pruet's lawyers advanced something we called the spigot theory, which meant when they turned off a spigot for one client, it was fine to turn on a spigot for another. This is absolutely *not* how legal representation works. We ended up settling the case for approximately $1.5 million, which in 2001 was an impressive amount of money and a very large legal malpractice settlement. Thanks to my friend from Camden, and a lot of hard work, Ronnie and I were off to the races.

We continued to build our practices in a number of legal areas, believing the legal malpractice case against Nexsen Pruet was a one-off. But less than two years later, we got a call from a guy named Frank Robertson, who was involved in the invention and patenting of a pecan nutcracking machine with his boss Bland Quantz, who owned the patent. The two split ways because Frank wanted to distribute the pecan nutcracking machines in Mexico and throughout South America, but Bland Quantz wanted no part of that kind of expansion. After the split, Frank was going to be Quantz's competitor to some degree, so he asked for legal counsel from—you guessed it—Nexsen Pruet. The firm wrote an opinion letter in which it was alleged that Frank was told that the patent at issue could not prohibit him from selling products in Mexico where he wanted to sell them. But we believed the opinion was incomplete and should have given Frank Robertson more warnings and advice about the possibilities of infringement.

He paid $15,000 for that opinion letter and, based on that legal advice, began selling pecan nutcracking machines in Mexico. These sales originated from his home office in Lexington, South Carolina. Frank had taught himself Spanish and developed a whole new market for the machine. While Frank believed the sales in Mexico were lawful based on the legal advice he'd received from Nexsen Pruet, this was not the case. After about two years of building a successful business, Bland Quantz sued Frank in federal court for patent infringement. Frank was confused and asked his lawyers at Nexsen Pruet to assist because they had written the very opinion letter that Frank contended had gotten him sued. He'd followed their counsel in the opinion letter. Nexsen Pruet filed an answer in the case but didn't raise the legal advice of counsel defense in the answer to the complaint because we alleged that they were covering up their own negligence. You see, the opinion letter that Frank had paid Nexsen Pruet to write did not explain that in order for the international sales to be "international" and not violate the US patent, every part of the sale had to take place *outside* US territory. So, when Frank was making sales on his phone from his home office in Lexington, South Carolina, he was unknowingly violating the patent even though the sales were being made to clients in Mexico and the machines were being shipped there.

Frank got sued, as he said in his own words, because "I followed my lawyers' advice." His former boss, Bland Quantz, had a legitimate claim. Once we were invited to get involved, we could see the problem right away. We couldn't believe we were going up against Nexsen Pruet in yet another legal malpractice suit. At a minimum, we asked the Nexsen Pruet team to give

Frank back his $15,000. They said they would but never did. Nexsen Pruet denied liability and argued that Frank did not follow their advice. As the case escalated, Nexsen Pruet had several opportunities to settle, but they didn't. Maybe they'd decided to use this case to bring down Bland Richter once and for all. So, in 2005, the case went to trial in Richland County for two weeks. And guess what? We got the largest jury verdict for a pure legal malpractice case in South Carolina history—$5.5 million. How did we do this? Well, this courtroom scene helped:

I asked Nexsen Pruet's lead patent attorney to take the stand.

"Did you bring your checkbook?"

"Sorry, what do you mean?" he asked.

"You know, your checkbook, because two years ago, you told us to tell Frank that you'd write him a $15,000 refund check for your flawed opinion letter. But you never did pay him back. The man paid you fifteen grand, and you gave him bad advice. Then, you admitted to giving him the wrong advice and said you'd give him his money back. If you could write him a check right now for the $15,000, please, in front of the jury, we'll just get that out of the way."

The lawyer refused, so I moved on.

"You wrote the opinion letter, correct?"

"Yes, I did," the patent attorney replied.

"And the client paid for that opinion letter, correct?"

"Yes, he did."

"And you're giving your client advice in the opinion letter, right?"

"Yes, that's right."

"And your client has a right to rely on that advice, correct?"

"Well . . ." he paused. "Sometimes . . ."

"Sometimes?" I was walking while I interrogated him and stopped in my tracks to face the witness box. "What do you mean by *sometimes*?"

"I mean that the client doesn't have the right to *always* rely on what I say."

The mood shifted instantly. It was like every ounce of air had been sucked out of the courtroom in an instant. No one could believe what they'd just heard this well-regarded, expert, highly compensated patent lawyer say. I looked over at Ronnie, and he gave me a look that said, "That's it!" I probably had another two hours of cross-examination scheduled for the patent attorney, but I looked over at the jury and their expressions said it all. They were aghast! A client doesn't always have the right to rely on what their lawyer advises after paying them $15,000 for an opinion?! That doesn't make any sense at all! We were now sure we were going to win—and win big—for our client Frank Robertson. When it came time for the jury to decide the verdict and a compensation amount, they actually asked the judge if there was a limit on the punitive damages they could reward—and the rest is history.

At the time, there was only one other lawyer who regularly handled legal malpractice cases in the state of South Carolina. His name was Cam Lewis, and his wife is now a United States district court judge. He was notorious for his rough-and-tumble methods as a litigator. Cam was a former West Point quarterback, and his father was a football coach at West Virginia University. He has since died and will forever enjoy a reputation as one of South Carolina's best litigators. Stepping into this professional gap, Bland Richter was on a roll—but we were also learning that we were entering into a world filled with shady people. A lot of our cases introduced us to the dark underbelly of South Carolina society. I'll never forget this hard-money lender we met during the Myrick vs. Nexsen Pruet case. Our client Jimmy Myrick and his potential business partner had considered borrowing money from this guy to buy a tomato farm so the land could be developed. This hard-money lender wanted everyone to know just how tough he was. Our clients told Ronnie and me the story about how one borrower from this hard-money lender had failed to pay him back on time, so the lender pushed the client into his truck, drove him to his barn, and tied his arms and legs to a chair. The borrower was petrified and sitting there sweating like a pig when this hard-money lender took out a blue marker and started drawing a line on the guy's bald head from his forehead all the way to the back of his neck—chuckling as he drew.

"What the hell are you doing?" the client asked.

The hard-money lender stopped drawing, looked the borrower right in the eyes, and said, "I'm drawing a line on your fucking head where I'm going to split it in two with an axe if you don't pay me back my money in one month."

These were the kinds of circles we'd started traveling in during the early days at Bland Richter. It wasn't pretty work, but it paid the bills. We quickly learned that when you sue lawyers, you're going to come face-to-face with some tough characters and have to learn how to play hardball without killing your career or losing your ticket to practice law. It was a balancing act. Luckily, my big, bodybuilder physique kept most people from messing with us.

Within five years, Bland Richter became known as a strong law firm willing to sue other lawyers or powerful law firms and hold them accountable for malpractice when it occurred, which we were discovering was much more often than we could have ever imagined. This reputation played well with clients but made us a lot of enemies in the legal community. At first, this took a toll on us. We had to get used to being disliked. After a while, this fueled us. We didn't care if they hated us as long as they respected us—and over time, they did, because we won a lot of cases and landed some big settlements. A few calls from other lawyers who were fed up with some of the bad representation they'd repeatedly seen from some of their colleagues started calling our offices with tip-offs. They wanted justice served while remaining anonymous. Pretty soon, we were bringing legal malpractice lawsuits or claims against some of the biggest law firms in the state, such as Nexsen Pruet, Nelson Mullins, McNair, Turner Padget, Motley Rice, Womble Carlyle, and others—including Jones Day, the largest law firm in the world at the time. We even had a third legal malpractice case against Nexsen Pruet. It was another case in which the firm was accused of giving our client a flawed patent opinion letter, and it resulted in a seven-figure settlement for our client.

After this third legal malpractice lawsuit against Nexsen Pruet, the firm went on the offensive with a huge, front-page article in *South Carolina Lawyers Weekly* titled "Nexsen Pruet's Nemesis" in October 2008. The article tried to paint us as a small firm that targeted good lawyers who worked at big firms like Nexsen Pruet. Maybe they thought the article would make us look bad, but it backfired big-time. The article was great for business at Bland Richter. We went on to bigger, more public cases that garnered national attention.

Interestingly, after many years of full-contact litigation between Nexsen Pruet and Bland Richter, the unexpected happened. Two of Nexsen Pruet's top litigators, Angus McCauley and Jimmy Long, became my friends. Angus and Jimmy are good and honorable lawyers who fight hard for their clients. In my younger years, I'd painted a broad brush over the law firm where they worked—but maybe I'd been too harsh. Maturity brings perspective. From where I sit today, I believe there are many more good lawyers at Nexsen Pruet than not. Every couple of months, Angus, Jimmy, and I go out to lunch to catch up on each other's lives. Never would my younger self have guessed this could be possible.

CHAPTER 10

FAMILY, WORK, AND GUIDING PRINCIPLES

"The winners are the ones who really
listen to the truth of their hearts."

—*Rocky Balboa*

A s I've mentioned, I grew up in a large, loving, traditional, extended Jewish family surrounded by siblings, grandparents, aunts, and uncles, as well as friends and neighbors who were like family. The house was rarely quiet, and we all loved it that way. There were always basketball games going on in the driveway or people gathered in the kitchen making or eating food. Everyone knew the rules and was expected to play their part to keep the family whole, secure, and healthy. We didn't have a lot of money, but we had a set of clear, guiding principles that inspired us to push ourselves to do our best and be good people.

As a kid, I dismissed and rebelled against these principles big-time. I think that was just the journey I had to take to fully understand their value. But as I've shared, I finally woke up and turned my life around—after almost killing myself by jumping off a fourth-story balcony in college, that is. It had taken two decades, but I began to live by the family principles I'd challenged as a kid. This shift brought about profound, positive change in my life. Not only was I much happier and healthier, but I was also much more successful. I liked how it felt to achieve my goals and be grateful for the abundance in my life rather than blame the world for what it hadn't given me, which was what I'd done all too often as a kid.

Around 2000, as my life and career entered the beginning of a new century, I was really hitting my stride. I had my own successful law firm with my wonderful law partner, Ronnie, whom I admired and respected. I was married to an amazing woman I adored and couldn't wait to get home to after work. Renée and I had been blessed with two children, who were running around all over the house teaching us all kinds of new and important things about life. Our daughter, now Dr. Sydney Bland, was born in 1995 and decided she wanted to be a doctor at the age of two. As I write this book, she's now in her general surgical residency at University of Alabama in Birmingham, with the goal of becoming a plastic surgeon. She is one of the hardest workers I've ever met, and I'm amazed at how much she has been willing to sacrifice to pursue her dreams. Our son, Davis, was born in 1997. He's an athlete just like his dad. He was the captain of his high school football team senior year and won the state SCISA football championship. He led the state with 155 tackles that year. He played football for a year at Wofford University, then transferred to University of South Carolina, where he graduated with a business degree. Davis now works for a publicly traded home builder as a senior financial analyst. I'm very proud of him. He's a great son and growing into a mature, responsible man. My life is filled with blessings, and I try to express my deep gratitude every day by paying it forward.

From the get-go, Renée and I wanted to raise our children to be strong, independent thinkers, high achievers, and good people. We worked daily to pass down the guiding principles that had shaped our lives. I definitely had a strong sense of urgency about this. Not only was I afraid I'd screw up parenthood, but I was also petrified my children might suffer through a period of bad behavior, as I had. I desperately wanted to save them from those torturous years. And I certainly didn't want them to treat their parents the way I'd treated mine. The stuff I'd put my dad through—oh, man! He really was a saint. When I lost my dad in 2015, after a tough, sixteen-year battle with multiple cancers, I remember thinking, *I wish I could get all those lost years back.* I didn't know any better as a kid, but once I did, I spent every day trying to make my dad proud. I've devoted my life to honoring the principles he instilled in me. Hopefully, somewhere in Heaven, he knows I'm sorry for making his life so hard and understands how grateful I am for all that he and my mother sacrificed to give me so many opportunities. He gave everything to his family because that's all that mattered to him. I am the product of my wonderful father—as are my two older brothers. He taught us to work hard and live a moral life. Even today, my father's spirit still guides me. I strive to do what's right in the world and be an agent for change because that's what he taught me to do.

I didn't want my children to have as many regrets as I did. On the other hand, I knew they'd have a much more privileged childhood than I'd had—and this made me nervous too. Having my kids feel entitled was not something I could stomach. This was the constant battle in my head: *How can I give my kids a good life without having them go soft? How can I make sure they don't screw things up before adopting life's transformative principles? Maybe I could make them a cheat sheet,* I thought. I also have this nagging concern that I could die before my kids find their true paths in life, but that's for a different book. So, with all this in mind, I started writing down the life principles that were important to me, that had guided me out of the darkness of my early years and into the light of my adult years. I also needed to articulate these principles more clearly for myself.

The task wasn't easy. I found that many of the principles were connected and needed to be explored together. I was challenged by the exercise but undeterred. There's a quote by President Theodore Roosevelt that has always stuck with me and captured the essence of what I was trying to articulate to myself and my children:

> It is not the critic who counts; not the man who points out how the strong man stumbles, or where the doer of deeds could have done them better. The credit belongs to the man who is actually in the arena, whose face is marred by dust and sweat and blood; who strives valiantly; who errs, who comes short again and again, because there is no effort without error and shortcoming; but who does actually strive to do the deeds; who knows great enthusiasms, the great devotions; who spends himself in a worthy cause; who at the best knows in the end the triumph of high achievement, and who at the worst, if he fails, at least fails while daring greatly, so that his place shall never be with those cold and timid souls who neither know victory nor defeat.

I don't want this to seem like a self-help book, but as my family and Bland Richter entered a new century, it was really important for me as a father, husband, and professional to figure out the principles, behaviors, and mindset that were driving my success. I wanted to explore why my life was so good and positive now and such a hot mess when I was a kid. The contrast was always with me—and I never wanted to slip back into my old ways. In the end, I came up with five principles. When my children were finally of school age, I would drive them in the morning, and we'd have about a twenty-minute ride together. Instead of listening to music, playing games, or having a casual chat, we used this time to discuss these five life principles. I know what you're thinking. *That's pretty heavy, Eric, they're just kids.* I get it, but you have to remember my overarching fear that they'd go off the rails like I had as a kid. To stay calm and grounded, I imparted this knowledge to my children as soon as possible and continued to internalize and practice all five principles myself.

PRINCIPLE 1: INVEST IN YOUR DREAMS AND IGNORE THE NOISE

No one gets a golden ticket in life—no one. Even if you're born into wealth and power, you still shape your own destiny. Look at Alex Murdaugh. He had both, and now he's in prison for life for double murder and as a result of a whole host of serious financial crimes. We either shape our destiny with the unique gifts God gave us, miss the boat, or worst of all, misuse our gifts like Murdaugh did, creating misery for himself, his family, and many others. Your personal decisions, *not* your circumstances, shape your destiny.

Only you, in all your uniqueness, can shape your distinct destiny through hard work, perseverance, curiosity, and drive. We are all called to contribute to this world differently, so keep learning and honing your unique talents. There will always be distractions as well as critics and naysayers. Ignore them; they are nothing more than noise and not worthy of your attention. Be like Teflon and let any negativity slide right off you. If you aren't ruffling any feathers, you probably aren't pushing the envelope hard enough. The key is not to wait for luck; go make your own. I always gently correct people when they wish me,

"Good luck!" I say, "Wish me 'good skills,' because if I use my skills effectively, the 'luck' will come."

Go through all the doors life opens for you. The future does not get delivered on a silver platter. It is shaped by your everyday choices, behaviors, and mindset. Believe in your potential and never stop moving toward your dreams. ABM—Always Be Moving! Falling and failing are part of the journey. It proves that you are in motion and making progress. Not much happens when you're standing still. No one ever reaches their full potential without getting really comfortable with failure, adversity, and challenges. These are our greatest teachers. In fact, in many ways, the ups and downs of the journey are more important than the destination. If you aren't moving forward, you are moving backward.

When I was young and troubled, I let the world shape me. I was directionless and let circumstances push me around. Then, I blamed the circumstances for my mistakes, instead of holding myself accountable. It wasn't until I found daily weight lifting as a teenager that I started to realize I could literally reshape my body and my life. I went from being a weak kid who hid to avoid bullies to a strong and powerful man who commanded respect. I went from being kicked out of school to being top of my class. This was the result of a simple decision to change my mindset and behaviors. I don't wait for things to happen. I make them happen through discipline, routine, and positive habits. That's what creates opportunity. I've really lived two lives—the life before I decided to invest in my dreams and the life after I made that decision. Hands down, I prefer the latter.

PRINCIPLE 2: DISCOVER, NURTURE, AND HARNESS YOUR UNIQUE SUPERPOWERS TO BE A DIFFERENCE MAKER

As the child of Jewish immigrant grandparents who had lived through the Russian pogroms and the Holocaust—and also as someone who was bullied and saw my father bullied at work—I became passionate about helping the mistreated, marginalized, and preyed upon. In many ways, this obsession shaped my career in malpractice—and ultimately led me on a collision course with one of South Carolina's biggest bullies, Alex Murdaugh. To some degree, the fear and adversity of my childhood became a superpower I harnessed to do more and better as an adult. I am never content, never satisfied, and never able to rest on my laurels. On my worst days, negativity and fear swirl around in my head and tell me I'm not capable, I don't belong, or I'm not worthy. But on my best days, I harness these thoughts and let them propel me forward at warp speed. I work harder and achieve more. I go further, faster.

Another unique curse turned into a gift is my mouth. Yes, the same mouth that got me into so much trouble as a kid has become one of my superpowers as a lawyer. My mouth is a weapon, and my words are the bullets. I can tell a story in a courtroom that compels a jury to act. I can effectively talk to the press and bring national attention to Bland Richter's legal cases and the clients we represent. I can speak for the defenseless and give them a voice when they have been wronged and have no voice. Keep your mouth moving and always be selling yourself and those you support. For me, it is selling for my clients.

We all have many unique gifts. Ironically, sometimes they can feel like curses. One doesn't typically think about fear and a big mouth as superpowers. I guess that's why this principle is about recognizing, nurturing, and harnessing your unique superpowers. This is what makes all the difference. I didn't recognize or value my unique talents as a kid because I was too busy hiding from bullies. Once I realized my unique talents, I began to hone and harness them. Unrecognized and unharnessed, my mouth and fears wreaked havoc on my life. It took self-awareness, discipline, and practice to harness them. To this day, I still have to be intentional about how I use my superpowers. I have strategies that help. For example, if I get triggered and start shooting off my mouth, Renée will tap me on the arm to gently remind me to chill out. It works like a dream. When I get all riled up in the courtroom or in meetings and start hammering too hard, Ronnie gives me a little signal so he can take over and ratchet things back down. The two of us have very different superpowers as lawyers. I'm the Northern sledgehammer who bludgeons the truth out of people, and Ronnie is death by a thousand perfectly placed razor cuts, all delivered with a smile and Southern charm. We're opposites, which is why we make the perfect team. Securing justice for our clients—who are often the victims of terrible crimes—is important to me. To do this, I need control of my superpowers.

If you want to be the change you wish to see in the world, as Mahatma Gandhi once said, you have to discover your unique superpowers, continuously hone them, and learn to harness them to achieve your goals and make the world a better place. Whenever

I discuss this topic, I'm always reminded of Liam Neeson's famous monologue in the 2009 movie *Taken*. Neeson plays the role of a devoted and determined father whose his daughter is kidnapped—and he is relentless in his pursuit of her safe return. Here's what he tells the kidnappers when they call for ransom money: "I don't know who you are. I don't know what you want. If you are looking for ransom, I can tell you I don't have the money. But what I do have are a very particular set of skills, skills I have acquired over a very long career, skills that make me a nightmare for people like you. If you let my daughter go now, that'll be the end of it. I will not look for you. I will not pursue you. But if you don't, I will look for you, I will find you, and I will kill you." Watch out, bad guys. That is the statement of a man who has complete confidence in and control over his superpowers and the unique skills he has obviously honed!

PRINCIPLE 3: CREATE THE REPUTATION YOU WANT

Don't let others create your reputation. Here's a hard truth: none of us have any control whatsoever over how others perceive us. Every human sees the world and other people through their own prism—and we can't control that prism. What we can control are our own actions, behaviors, habits, words, and thoughts. If all these are productive and consistent, people will take notice. Of course, as Taylor Swift sings, "The haters gonna hate . . ." but that's just noise, and we've already decided to tune out the noise. The people who count are the ones who notice your behaviors and form opinions. Does Eric keep his word? Does Eric give it his all? Does Eric treat others with respect? Is Eric prepared? Is Eric on time? Does Eric follow through? The answers to these questions shape your reputation. People are always observing, assessing, and deciding how to interact with you based on answers to those questions. If the answer is consistently "yes," people will interact with you much more constructively than if the answer is "sometimes" or "no." I know this firsthand.

When I was a kid, I had a reputation as a troublemaker, loudmouth, and class clown. This reputation was consistent with my behaviors and actions. I earned my reputation. I caused a lot of trouble and was always goofing off in class. I sought to be the center of attention through pranks and jokes. As a lawyer, I developed a reputation as a bulldog because I was a fierce legal opponent and relentless in my pursuit of justice for my clients. Again, this reputation fits my habits, style, and behaviors. As you can see, I changed my reputation quite dramatically between childhood and adulthood. So, if you're not happy with your reputation at work, home, or in your community, it's never too late. I'm living proof of this. But remember, your reputation is a sacred trust. A reputation is hard work to obtain, and it's hard work to maintain. You've got to keep walking the talk to sustain a stellar reputation.

Because of our blue-collar backgrounds, Ronnie and I built reputations as hardworking lawyers with a laser-like focus on our clients. We listen carefully and respectfully to the people who come to Bland Richter. We are honored to be entrusted with their legal matters. Once we fully understand a client's issues, we go into battle for them with a strong sense of urgency and commitment we believe is unique in our profession.

PRINCIPLE 4: PREPARE FOR A STRONG START AND FINISH

This principle is about all the little daily habits that set me up for success. They fall into four buckets: preparation, organization, strong start, and strong finish. These habits can effectively help you get through your day, run a meeting, raise your kids, complete a race or a test, or even prepare a meal—you name it, the approaches in each of these buckets can help. Preparation and organization might seem obvious. If you are failing to prepare for success, you are preparing to fail. Everyone knows that if you have a meeting and you want it to go well, you have to prepare for it. Maybe it takes an hour or two, but you get ready. But I look at preparation a bit differently. I think of preparation as more of a continuum. If you want to be healthy, you have to buy healthy food (not keep a lot of junk food in the house), cook healthy food (choose the right ingredients), and eat healthy food. Then, you have to work out. These small but significant behavioral changes prepare the way for you to be healthy. In this case, preparation is not just for an hour or two before an event—which is how we so often think about preparation—rather, it's a form of continuous training and habit creation that paves the way for better outcomes and a better life. I am not a crammer or a last-minute guy. You can't do your best work when you're rushed. Figure out what needs to be accomplished and start doing those things right away on a regular basis. Preparation is a lifestyle and mindset in which you are constantly preparing for better things to come. Of course, being organized about your preparation helps tremendously. Are you blocking off the time you need to go purchase and prepare healthy food? Do you make a list before you go to the store, so you come back with what you need? You get my drift. Organization is the foundation of preparation, and preparation is the foundation of positive behaviors and habits.

My personal fear of failure, which is an ever-present companion, keeps me in continuous preparation mode. It can be exhausting, and maybe some would say it's too much—or even extreme or unhealthy. But it's who I am, and I can tell you it has a lot of benefits, because I'm always ready for life's surprises and opportunities. In my mind, this is a positive. If you are constantly preparing for your dreams to come true, you have a much better chance of making them happen because you are fully prepared when your big break comes. You're ready to take advantage of the moment. This is something overachievers practice every day. Never stop preparing to make your dreams come true.

As for the starting and finishing, both should be strong, of course. But don't forget the in-between because that is where you must grind. Starting strong means you never come out of the gate without being ready to bring your all to the moment. I don't ease into anything; it's foot on the gas immediately. Whether it's your morning routine or a pregame (or in my case a pretrial) ritual, it means you have the energy, mindset, resources, tools, and people in place to get to the head of the pack fast. You can't start strong without being prepared and organized, so these concepts are all intertwined. Starting strong means setting the tone. People take notice and pay attention when you start strong, and this creates momentum, which is crucial at the beginning of anything. Starting strong also means you bring all the energy of your vision, your belief in yourself, and your dreams to the moment. You're ignoring the noise and are laser focused on the task at hand. You are fully present. That's why I eliminate distractions from my life. I keep my life skinny. All of this has an impact on outcomes, so it's very important to start strong.

Finishing strong, on the other hand, is about commitment, integrity, and excellence. It means you've overcome all the challenges and roadblocks along the way in order to achieve your goal. There's a reason runners say races are won or lost in the last mile, because that's when you've stretched your mind and body to their limits and are calling upon all final reserves to get you across the finish line. One of my favorite lines is, "There is no traffic jam on the extra mile." It's when all the training, endurance, habit formation, and mindset work comes into play. A lot of people can come out of the gate strong, but it's the people who finish strong who get the job done. Execution is everything. There's very little value to starting strong if you can't finish strong as well. Be prepared to deliver both—and with excellence. You'll see your reputation soar.

PRINCIPLE 5: DO WHAT IS RIGHT, NOT WHAT IS POPULAR

When I was a kid, I just wanted to fit in. I wanted everyone to like me. I wanted to be part of the "in" crowd. It's a pretty common trap for insecure people. I let others set the bar, and I jumped as high as I could hoping they would like me, let me hang out with them, and protect me from the bullies. It didn't work out too well for me, and I wasted a lot of years listening to the noise. I cared too much about how others saw me and too little about how I saw myself. I cared too much about being accepted and not enough about being respected. I was drifting around trying to be popular when I should have focused on being a better person. It took a near-death experience to snap me out of this negative pattern. Now, so many years later, I can honestly say I am grateful for that frightening experience my freshman year in college because it put me on the right course.

Early in my law career, I still struggled with insecurity, mostly because I was so different than my colleagues. I was Jewish. I didn't graduate from an Ivy League school. I didn't have the right pedigree or connections. I let fear and self-doubt get the best of me. I reminded myself daily that I wasn't as accomplished as my brothers. I wasn't as smart. I was a screwup. You name it, and I was beating myself up for it. But somewhere along the way, I found my backbone and hit my stride. My mission to get justice for my clients started to outweigh my desire to be liked and my need to beat myself up. I was up against people who were doing bad things to good people, and I wanted to give voice to the victims and stop the bad behavior. I started to recognize the outsider's advantage and care less about my popularity and more about doing the right thing. Honestly, at the time, this approach didn't seem to be in vogue in South Carolina's legal community. This would change over time, in no small part because of what was revealed during the Murdaugh trial.

If you do what's right, you'll always be able to respect yourself and earn the respect of others. This is all that matters. Being liked is fleeting. But to be respected, you have to be tough when necessary. Being respected doesn't happen all at once. It takes time. Remember, I was part of Senator Dick Harpootlian's elite inner circle until I stood up to him and his cronies for bullying my friend Ronnie. It was rough going in the beginning, but it was the right thing to do. And look where it got me! Ronnie is now my partner, and we're a great team. If I'd kowtowed to Harpootlian's demands just to be liked by and remain part of his powerful inner circle, I wouldn't be part of Bland Richter, and I wouldn't be the successful lawyer I am today. Do what is right, even if it's not popular. Being liked isn't worth it. Respect, on the other hand, is timeless and is the foundation of trust—and trust is necessary to build meaningful relationships with the good people who can help you achieve your dreams.

As my children, Sydney and Davis, grew older and started to face some of the normal preteen and teen social pressures—as well as those created by my line of work—these five principles served as a kind of armor to shield them from the worst of it. When Ronnie and I broke the unwritten rule that lawyers should never sue other lawyers, things got pretty ugly—first in the courtroom and then socially in our community. This impacted us and our families.

I remember Ronnie and I going down to a status conference in the Lowcountry for one of our cases. Ironically, this was the county where the Murdaugh saga would later take place. But this status conference was after our big jury verdict and settlements against Nexsen Pruet and other law firms. Judge Buckner asked us back to his chambers, where Ronnie and I sat on one side of the room and a couple of local lawyers sat on the other. The judge started yucking it up with these lawyers for a good fifteen minutes. They were just ten feet away from us but acted like we weren't there. Ronnie and I sat quietly and respectfully, waiting for them to finish. The entire time, the judge never even looked at us. Ronnie and I had driven two hours for this status conference, so when their conversation hit the forty-minute mark, I finally spoke up.

"Excuse me, Judge, are we going to get to the status conference?"

All the laughter across the room stopped, and the judge slowly turned toward Ronnie and me. "We'll start when I'm ready," he said seriously in his deep Southern accent.

He glared at us like we were pariahs for a minute, then turned back to the other lawyers and kept talking for a few more minutes.

Finally, he turned back to us. "So, you two are the lawyers who make a living suing other lawyers. You can't make a decent living any other way? Really? You gotta make your livelihood suing other lawyers?"

Now we knew where we stood. We muddled through the status conference and headed back home fully aware of the kind of toxic courtroom environment we were likely to face going forward. Legal malpractice was clearly new to the state, and it was not being received well by the powers that be.

But the ugliness wasn't contained to the courtroom and legal circles. In the early 2000s, the population of Columbia was only about 122,000, so it was considered a small city. To give you some perspective, it was only a quarter of the size of Atlanta. Columbia has grown like wildfire since, but back then, social circles were pretty small. If you were a lawyer, those circles got even smaller. My kids went to different private schools. Sydney went to Hammond, and Davis went to Heathwood. These were the schools where most of the successful lawyers and physicians sent their kids. And there I was suing some of these lawyers and physicians. As you can imagine, it could get a little rough for my kids. When we'd attend a sporting event, we'd sit off on our own. When someone would find out that Sydney or Davis's last name was Bland, they'd hear things like, "Oh, you're Bland's kid. Why is your father suing my dad? You suck!" My family wasn't invited to a lot of events or parties, and my kids were sometimes excluded as well. Some days were harder to deal with than others. I'd remind Sydney and Davis over and over not to listen to the noise, not to give any weight to the negative comments.

"We do what's right in the Bland house," I'd say, "not what's popular. It's not always the easiest path, but for us it's the only one, the right one." These words were my dad talking through me. He had shared a similar message with me and my brothers when we were kids.

In theory, they understood, but it was a lot for two young people to handle, and Renée and I knew this. We worked hard to fortify them and make our home and family a haven where our kids could feel accepted and heard. Amid all the social tensions, we were also trying to raise good, decent human beings. We wanted our kids to work hard, excel in the classroom and beyond, stay organized, be honest and respectful, be on time, and so forth—all the big and small life skills you want your children to master so they can actually go out in the world someday and make it on their own. But the world Renée and I were parenting in was so much more sheltered than what either of us had known as kids. We were so much more involved in our children's lives than our parents had been in ours. It seemed to be the modern way, but sometimes we both questioned whether it was the best thing for our kids. For all my flaws as a teen, I was very capable of taking care of myself. I could get myself across town on a crowded train or bus at fourteen. I was fiercely independent. There was no hand-holding, no hovering. My parents didn't have time for any of that, and maybe that was a good thing. My kids were driven everywhere and dropped at the front door. I wondered whether they'd be able to navigate the real world.

In parenting, Renée and I had very different styles. Surprise, I can be very intense. It's just who I am and how I was raised. Remember, on my good days, my fears are my super-power, but on my worst days, they are my nemesis, making me question and doubt everything—even my children. Then there's that mouth of mine—so powerful in the courtroom and in front of the press but a loaded weapon in a house with kids. There were days I struggled to navigate the shift from a stressful day of lawyering and grilling witnesses in the court-room and in depositions to being a calm, understanding, lev-elheaded husband and father at home. I know I'm not alone in this struggle, and I've worked hard to harness these forces to give my family the best of me, instead of the worst. I have always been so hard on myself, which causes me to be uninten-tionally hard on those around me. My issues have sometimes expressed themselves in surprising ways, especially with my son. I am competitive to a fault, especially at golf and weight lifting. I always have to do my best. I am a six handicap at golf. I was too competitive with my son when he was growing up. We competed at everything—basketball, golf, weight lifting, sports and Seinfeld trivia, you name it. I would not let him beat his old man. It created tension in our relationship, and I'm forever sorry for letting my competitive spirit get the best of me. As I've said, life is a journey of continuous improvement. As soon as I became aware of my negative behavior, I tried to change it. As always, I am a work in progress.

Because we were all committed to making our family a haven, we always worked through our differences and found common ground. One family activity that really helped was ski-ing. We've gone skiing together every year since 2002. My brother Richie lives in Stowe, Vermont, and we would visit him during the holidays every year. When Sydney was seven and Davis was five, my brother said, "Why don't I take you four skiing?" We started on the bunny slope and by the end of the week were going down slightly more challenging trails. We were hooked.

Every year since, we have continued to ski for a minimum of three weeks together every year. It is something we look all forward to. We bought a four-week timeshare in Aspen, Colorado, and we can all do almost any run there—on or off the trails. Skiing together all these years has brought us closer as a family. The talks we've had going up the chairlift never would have taken place elsewhere. We really open up to one another. It has been a godsend. Hopefully, my kids will teach their children to ski, and we'll be able to continue this wonderful tradition with our grandkids someday. We ski fast and hard and constantly challenge ourselves. We usually ski more than twenty thousand vertical feet a day and do between fifteen to twenty runs. It's hard on the body and has ultimately taken a toll on my knees, but it has been worth it to scoop up my family and escape from the noise of daily life into the eternal beauty and healing quiet of the snowy mountains.

Me in my basketball uniform in ninth grade. I was the proverbial 98-pound weakling who had other people fight his battles for him. I now fight my own battles.

*Me, Renee, and my dad with the kids. Fitness
became a lifesaving focus for me.*

My life transformed when I took control of my health and mindset. I was a first year law student and the USC football program sent me down to Florida to chaperone the players.

Bodybuilding was the path to the discipline and confidence I was seeking and something I would carry with me for the rest of my life.

The dollar I received from my first legal malpractice case after betting opposing counsel I would prevail on behalf of my client. This dollar reminds me to always bet on myself.

SOUTH CAROLINA
LAWYERS WEEKLY

M DOLAN MEDIA COMPANY

http://www.sclawyersweekly.com

| Vol. 8, No. 6 | Oct. 6, 2006 | $7.00 per copy | Columbia, S.C. |

Nexsen Pruet's nemesis?

Duo files fourth malpractice suit against large firm

BY RICK BRUNDRETT
Special to South Carolina Lawyers Weekly

The two law firms couldn't be much more opposite.

One is the third largest firm in South Carolina, with more than 160 lawyers at five offices in Columbia, Charleston, Greenville, Hilton Head Island and Myrtle Beach, plus two more in North Carolina.

Its gleaming downtown Columbia headquarters, housed in a bank skyscraper, sits kitty-corner to the S.C. Supreme Court with a view of the State House across the street. Founded in 1945, the firm represents some of the biggest corporations in South Carolina and the U.S.

The other firm is a two-man show based out of an older house in Columbia's north downtown area, with a second office in Charleston.

The 11-year-old partnership has concentrated on commercial disputes and medical and professional malpractice cases. Its Web site proudly proclaims seven- and eight-figure verdicts and settlements obtained on behalf of unnamed clients.

But despite their outward differences, the Bland Richter and Nexsen Pruet firms are very well acquainted.

This is when Bland Richter was announced as "Nexsen Pruet's Nemesis." It was the dawn of a new era in my law career. This article told us we were now living rent free in Nexson Pruitt's head.

125

Renee and I with President Joe Biden and his wife Jill. These are some of the many incredible people I've had the pleasure to meet during my career. Ironically, this was a fundraising event hosted at Dick Harpootlian's home.

Renee and I with President Bill Clinton at Allen University in Columbia, SC. Lots of miles since then, and a few grays.

Professional wrestler and former client Ric Flair. To become friends with my childhood hero was one of the highlights of my life. Flair taught me the importance of telling your own story—rather than letting others tell it for you.

#freedomfighters
#justiceforzachhammon
#alllivesmatter

FREEDOM
FIGHTER

Justice for Zachary Hammond!

I was able to put heat on the police department and city of Seneca in the wrongful shooting and death case of Zachary Hammond by having multiple press conferences where the national media was in attendance—along with Zachary's parents, Angie and Paul Hammond.

My incredible father. He was the best man at my wedding and has always been my moral compass.

My best friend, Danny Snelgrove.

*Murdaugh victim Brian Satterfield. It was an emotional turn
for me when I recognized the depth of Alex Murdaugh's deceit.
I was committed to getting justice for these incredible people.*

This is a photo of Gloria Satterfield and her son Tony, which shows the love and happiness between them. She did not die in vain, as her death led to the downfall of the Murdaugh dynasty. She was so much more than the references to her as "the Murdaugh's housekeeper" during the trial.

This hug was right before Tony Satterfield was brave enough to testify in front of the world at Alex Murdaugh's murder trial. Representing the Satterfield family has been one of the great honors of my career.

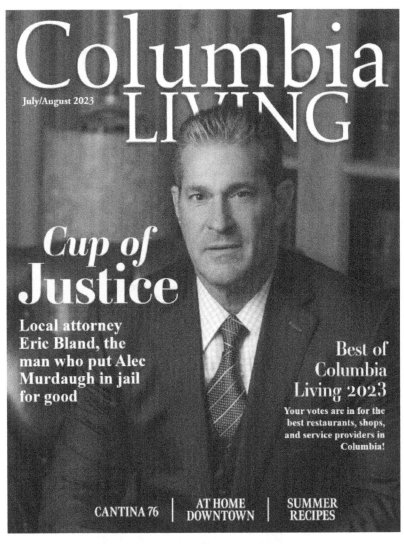

July/August 2023

Columbia LIVING

Cup of Justice

Local attorney
Eric Bland, the
man who put Alec
Murdaugh in jail
for good

Best of Columbia Living 2023

Your votes are in for the
best restaurants, shops,
and service providers in
Columbia!

CANTINA 76 | AT HOME DOWNTOWN | SUMMER RECIPES

*The Murdaugh trial brought intense media attention,
both locally and nationally. This story was a look behind
the impact the case had on our lives. It was also when
the world got to know my incredible wife Renee.*

The media has had a significant role in my career.
They are incredible allies in a shared demand
for transparency and accountability.

Here's the team: EB, Ronnie Richter, and Scott Mongillo.
Vulture Culture at its finest.

Skiing has been one of my family's greatest escapes.
It's how we love to spend time together as a family.
We've gone skiing every year since 2004.

My parents and my wife Renee have been the
most meaningful support systems in my life.

My courtroom confrontation with Alex Murdaugh.

My wife Renee and my daughter Sydney, the most amazing women in the world to me.

I love playing golf with my son Davis. It's always competitive.

*Enjoying time together with my son Davis at the
2024 US Open in Pinehurst, North Carolina.*

My beautiful mother. People say that we look like twins.
I take that as a compliment. She and my father sacrificed
so much to get me and my brothers where we are today.

My older brother Robbie and me. He has been a constant source of inspiration and support in my life. Here we are sharing a meal right before I accompanied my fellow United Homes Group board of directors for the NASDAQ ringing of the bell in May of 2023.

My middle brother Richie and me.

Renee and I with Murdaugh Murders Podcast fan and guest, Sheryl Crow. It was incredible meeting her and seeing the podcast's impact in the most unexpected of places.

My beloved parents.

My rock, my wife, and best friend, Renee.

Our "Pups of Justice" bring so much joy to our lives.

My beautiful daughter, a surgeon, Dr. Sydney A. Bland.

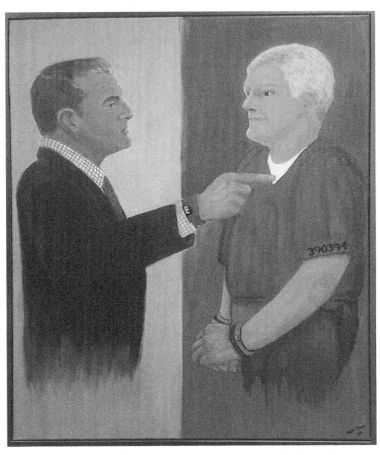

Throughout the Murdaugh matters, my "Cup Of Justice" and "Good Skill" podcast listeners sent me paintings, handmade gifts, and meaningful momentos. Painted by local South Carolina artist Stephanie Tryon, this artwork hangs outside of my office conference room. It captures perfectly the many battles between Alex Murdaugh and me over the last few years.

Forever grateful for the brilliant journalists and producer who ignited a global phenomenon and changed the course of our lives. Cups Up.

My friend, cohost, and unstoppable force Mandy Matney.

*My client Sandy Smith and her beloved son
Stephen. Our fight for justice will never end.*

CHAPTER 11

MY BEST FRIEND
IS A FELON

"If you are still breathing, you have a second chance."

—*Oprah Winfrey*

Our guiding principles and mounting successes continued to bring the Bland Richter law firm more and more interesting and high-profile cases as the 2000s unfolded. We represented underwater archaeologist Edward Lee Spence in a legal dispute with bestselling adventure novelist and underwater explorer Clive Cussler, who claimed that he, not Spence, had discovered the Confederate submarine *H. L. Hunley* off the coast of Charleston, South Carolina. The famous submarine was the first in history to sink an enemy warship. After claiming that he'd discovered the sub in 1995 and seeking to disprove Spence's claim of finding the Hunley in 1970, Cussler finally filed motions to dismiss a federal lawsuit against Spence in August of 2008. Just a week earlier, we had been told to prepare for trial. It was a win for Spence, who had been battling Cussler for seven years.

We also had a growing roster of well-known athletes in professional football (Corey Miller), golf (Brian Gay, Glen Day, and Kevin Kisner), hockey (David Shaw), and ice-skating (Tara Lipinski). We filed a wrongful death suit on behalf of the family of former University of South Carolina football coach Jim Carlen. I also represented banker André Lewis, who was accused and ultimately convicted of some of the charges in a money laundering jury trial that also accused sports agent William "Tank" Black Jr. of misappropriating funds from Heisman Trophy winner Charles Woodson of the Oakland Raiders, Washington Redskins running back Stephen Davis, and Dallas Cowboys quarterback Quincy Carter as well as Jamie Watson and Corey Jenkins. Probably the biggest of these sports clients was my childhood idol, professional wrestler and sixteen-time world champion Ric Flair, known as "Nature Boy." We litigated a trademark infringement matter on his behalf and helped him negotiate his wrestling obligations directly with legendary professional wrestling promoter Vince McMahon at the World Wrestling Entertainment's (WWE) palatial offices in Greenwich, Connecticut. Regarded by many as the greatest professional wrestler of all time, Flair's career had spanned more than fifty years. Working with Flair was a great time. With his fame and larger-than-life personality, people cheered us on wherever we went. He was a good client who became a great friend. He even taught me his signature move—the figure-four leg lock.

We had other high-profile cases as well, such as representing singer James Brown's manager in the James Brown estate fight. We represented former police officer Michael Slager, who was convicted of shooting and killing Walter Scott in North Charleston, South Carolina, during a chase, against the Police Benevolent Association in connection with their obligation to pay for Mr. Slager's criminal defense attorneys in the murder and civil rights criminal charges. We were able to resolve that litigation to Mr. Slager's satisfaction. We garnered the reputation as "hired guns." In fact, during one meeting in which we were being interviewed to represent a very successful businessman in a legal malpractice case over a contract for millions of dollars to replace computer and network systems in a large school district, the client walked into our offices, put a .44 Magnum on the table and said, "I am here to hire a gunslinger to get me what I am entitled to."

Though I made a lot of enemies due to the litigious nature of my work, I also forged a lot of strong friendships along the way, like with Ric Flair, who became more than just a client to me. Once again, my friends didn't run in the same social circles as the rest of the lawyers I knew. Their friends were mostly other lawyers. This wasn't the case for me at all. Outside of Ronnie and a handful of legal colleagues, such as close friend Chuck Thompson, my friends came from every walk of life *except* law. In fact, to this day, my best friend is a felon. No, you didn't misread that. My best friend is a convicted felon. You see, my father taught me that everyone is allowed to make mistakes. I was very grateful he felt this way because I'd made *a ton* of them when I was young.

"Don't judge people for their mistakes," my father would say. "Judge them based on how they react and what they do when they find out they've made a mistake. Do they accept responsibility or throw blame on others? How they act *after* the mistake tells you what kind of people they *really* are."

There is a famous saying that there is nothing to be learned from the second kick of a mule. So true. In life, you can't learn until you feel the pain. Some of the best life lessons are learned through mistakes. No one is perfect. If they say they are, they are not living close enough to the edge or they are just lying. They're not taking enough risks. A life fully lived is about taking risks, making mistakes, and then dusting yourself off and moving forward so you don't make that same mistake again. This had been the story of my life—a story of second chances—so my father's sage advice always stuck with me. As such, when I met anybody new, I always kept an open mind—as was the case when I met Danny Snelgrove in 2009. A mutual friend, a personal trainer named Ken Taylor, who was a former Mr. Universe, was training Danny at the time, and he said we should meet because we had so much in common.

"You both train hard," Ken said. "You're both golfers. You need to train together." We were introduced and hit it off immediately. Danny owned a successful fleet-truck maintenance business that serviced heavy-duty diesel trucks. He was a 285-pound monster of a man from all the weight lifting. His nickname was Diesel, or Big D for short.

About a month into our friendship, Danny said, "Eric, I need to tell you something."

"Sure," I said. "I'm listening."

Danny proceeded to tell me the most extraordinary story about how in the early 2000s, he, his lovely wife, Cindy, and their two children, Jewell and Danuel, were in New York City on vacation. They were attending a Broadway show when Danuel, who was eleven years old at the time, collapsed on the sidewalk outside the theater and had a seizure. They gave Danuel some water, calmed him down, and chalked it up as a strange anomaly. Danuel was very athletic and played AAU basketball. The next day, Danuel had another seizure, so they immediately left New York, came back to South Carolina, and sought medical treatment. The local physicians in Columbia diagnosed Danuel with intractable epilepsy and told the Snelgroves there was no cure. They then took Danuel to MUSC (Medical University of South Carolina in Charleston), where CAT scans confirmed the epilepsy diagnosis. For the next couple of years, Danuel suffered from numerous seizures that impacted his schooling and participation in AAU basketball.

The Snelgroves were not satisfied with the medical opinions about Danuel's condition.

Cindy, who is brilliant, began researching similar medical cases and found a brain specialist at Wayne State University in Detroit, Michigan, who she thought might have a treatment for her son's medical problems, which were worsening. The doctor at Wayne State used insane amounts of radiation to map Danuel's brain and discovered a tangled collection of blood vessels in one of his parietal lobes, which are the part of the brain responsible for receiving and processing sensory input. If not treated and removed, the doctor said, these tangled blood vessels would eventually grow into a tumor. However, to reach this area of the brain, a surgeon would have bypass key areas that controlled motor and speech abilities.

A neurosurgeon at the Miami Children's Hospital was recommended for the intricate and risky procedure. The cost? Hundreds of thousands of dollars. But the Snelgroves' health insurers told them the procedure was considered too experimental to warrant coverage. Danny and Cindy didn't have this kind of money, but like any loving parents, they would not be deterred. They were committed to saving their son's life. They would use their life savings and other funds and find a way to pay for this crucial treatment.

Danny started amassing debt and fell behind on his company's payroll and sales tax payments. Ultimately, he was forced to file for bankruptcy. During the bankruptcy proceedings, discrepancies were uncovered around nonpayroll distributions and compensation Danny was taking from his business to pay for his son's treatment. We all know how this story ends. Certainly, as a lawyer, I've seen these types of tragic cases many times. Danny was criminally charged with multiple financial felonies. Rather than go to trial and risk convictions that would incarcerate him for decades, Danny was advised by a well-regarded criminal attorney to plead guilty. The sentencing guidelines in his case indicated he'd probably spend four or five years in prison.

When Danny appeared in federal court for his sentence hearing, the judge asked, "Mr. Snelgrove, do you have any remorse for your crimes?" Danny was supposed to say yes to invoke the court's mercy. Instead, he responded, "No, Your Honor, I do not. I don't regret anything I have done for my son and family. I did these things to save my son's life, and I would do them all over again." In a stroke of divine intervention, the judge shared that she also had a sick family member and understood the desire to do everything possible for a loved one during a medical crisis. However, she added that the court must punish Danny for breaking the law. In light of the circumstances, and the fact that Danny had never broken the law before, the judge did indeed show mercy and sentenced him to serve one year and one day in federal prison. It was a miracle.

Equally miraculous was the fact that Danuel's treatments and multiple surgeries worked. Despite the odds, he was cured. In the middle of everything, young Danuel had promised his brain surgeon that if he were cured, he'd become a brain doctor too. Everyone smiled except Danuel. He was serious. So here is the extraordinary ending of this extraordinary story of love and commitment. Danny's son, Danuel, went on to graduate from the University of South Carolina School of Medicine and is now a renowned, board-certified critical care neurologist and associate professor at the Medical University of South Carolina in Charleston. He is thirty-eight years old and married, with two lovely children. That is why I couldn't be prouder to say that my best friend, Danny, is a felon. We do everything together, and so do our wives. We've been friends for fourteen years, and I can't imagine my life without Big D in it.

*   *   *

My father's advice to not judge people by their mistakes would influence me throughout my life, and in 2015, it played a major role in a pivotal case in my career. That year, Ronnie and I were brought into the homicide case of nineteen-year-old Zachary Hammond. When I was told Zachary was a bad kid, I didn't judge. I just listened. Zachary had caused his devoted parents, Angie and Paul Hammond, no small amount of grief. But that was nothing compared to the grief they felt when they received a call that their teenage son had been shot and killed by a police officer outside a Hardee's in Seneca, South Carolina. Officials told the Hammonds that Zachary had been shot twice in the chest while trying to flee the scene of a crime. Authorities told the Hammonds that their son had driven his car straight toward a cop named Mark Tiller, who'd been called to the scene to arrest Zachary for trying to sell drugs to an undercover cop. The official story was that the officer had frozen in front of Zachary's car and would have been run over had he not shot their son point-blank in the chest. It seemed like the police officer had no choice, and he was immediately cleared of all wrongdoing.

A couple of days after the incident, I got a phone call from Paul Hammond's relative and a client of mine, Dr. Thomas McFadden, a plastic surgeon in Greenville, South Carolina. Tom told me about Zachary's death. It seemed tragic.

"Eric," he said, "we don't think Zachary's death happened the way the authorities told us it did."

I listened to the details surrounding Zachary's death with an open mind and was intrigued. Not only did Zachary remind me a bit of the troubled kid I used to be, but something about the whole story the Hammonds had been told about their son's death just seemed off. Ronnie and I made an appointment with the coroner and drove down to Seneca the next day to view the body. The moment we entered the morgue, and the body bag was opened, Zachary's body told a very different story from the official version. It was immediately clear that the boy had been shot from behind, in the back, not from the front, as was reported. What we were looking at in the morgue was clearly not a direct frontal shot. We immediately asked for a complete autopsy and filed a lawsuit calling for evidence in the shooting to be released. This included the body cam footage.

As the facts started to unfold, we learned that thirty-two-year-old Lieutenant Mark Tiller, the officer who had shot Zachary, was allegedly a pumped-up, loudmouthed monster of a cop who had escaped disciplinary action many times. As is often the way with troubled cops, he'd been washed down from several larger police departments for getting in fights and other troublesome behavior. Tiller's record, much of which had been covered up, indicated he was a lit fuse who'd landed in the town of Seneca because local law enforcement couldn't find enough cops who wanted to work in such a small, rural town. Not Tiller—he was all in. He'd bragged in a weekly law enforcement meeting, "I'm gonna shoot somebody before I am done." It seemed he couldn't wait for an opportunity to draw his gun. Unfortunately, Zachary Hammond became Lieutenant Tiller's opportunity.

The Hammonds and Tori Morton, the young woman who'd been on a first date with Zachary the night of his shooting, helped Ronnie and me start to pull together all the puzzle pieces of that fateful evening, one unsettling fact at a time. Yes, Zachary was a messed-up kid who did drugs. But he wasn't a drug dealer moving around quantities of narcotics. He was just a stupid, cocky teenager trying to sell a single joint to a stranger. The kid wasn't as bad as he portrayed himself. He claimed to be a gang member, but he wasn't. Who knows why he was trying to look tougher than he was? Unfortunately, as Zachary headed to the Hardee's on July 26, 2015, he plugged in the wrong phone number, inadvertently texting a state trooper instead of the kid who was supposed to buy the joint. The trooper contacted local police, who decided to set up a sting operation to catch Zachary selling what they thought would be a whole bunch of marijuana and maybe other drugs, instead of the single joint.

When Zachary arrived at the Seneca Hardee's with Tori, he had no idea there was a plainclothes, undercover cop ready to buy the joint and arrest him. The minute the deal was closed, Lieutenant Tiller flew into the Hardee's parking lot, driving around fifty miles an hour and definitely out of control. He was ready to assist with the arrest and kick some ass. Zachary saw what was unfolding, got scared, and tried to flee the scene with Tori. Zachary put his car in reverse to pull out of their parking space. Tiller jumped out of his police car, immediately drew his gun, and pointed it directly at Zachary while he ran alongside the car, which was now in drive and pulling away. Unable to stop the boy from escaping, Tiller shouted, "Stop! Stop! Or I will shoot your fucking ass!" He then fired two shots into the kid's back and shoulder. Zachary was killed almost instantly. When other police officers arrived on the scene, Tiller enthusiastically told them, "I got one! I shot him!"

While some local South Carolina press covered the case, there was no national press attention. This sort of surprised me, as Zachary's murder happened at a time when a significant number of unarmed boys and men were being shot by cops. There was a national spotlight on the problem—and nationwide outrage. In 2014 to 2015 alone, there had been the Laquan McDonald shooting in Illinois, the Tamir Rice and Samuel DuBose cases in Ohio, the Eric Garner shooting in New York, the Michael Brown killing by police officers in Ferguson, Missouri, and the Walter Scott shooting in North Charleston, South Carolina. All of these cases had involved white cops killing young Black boys or men. But it seemed that the national press corps wasn't interested in Zachary Hammond's murder because it was a white-on-white shooting. This didn't sit right with me, so I got on the local news and said my piece.

"You know what? This is a disgrace. Where is everybody? Where's Al Sharpton? Where's Jesse Jackson? Where are all the protesters? If this had been a young Black man, there wouldn't be a hotel room available in the upstate of South Carolina. Why doesn't anybody care about Zachary Hammond?"

The press got the message, and word spread. The national press finally started picking up the story. I was interviewed about the case in the ensuing months by Anderson Cooper on CNN, Nancy Grace, Dr. Drew, and Dr. Phil. Our press conferences started to draw national newspaper and television reporters. Ronnie and I were always very prepared for these events with plenty of diagrams about how the bullets entered Zachary's body and other important facts about the case. I began to realize the value and power of the press—and it was game changing.

Most lawyers are afraid of the press, but I *love* the press! They are my friends, and I trust them. As long as you're honest with them and they're honest with you, it's a symbiotic relationship. You must be careful when you are specifying "on" or "off" the record. Zachary's case became a very public, national case—a first for our firm. Ronnie and I made a strong argument that it was time for the press to start covering white-on-white shootings that involved cops because it was a problem too.

The other message I had for the press—and this one was quite personal for me—had to do with Zachary's reputation as a bad kid. People wanted to dismiss the case because Zachary had been caricatured as a miscreant. The narrative that was gaining traction was that this kid was so bad, it was okay to eliminate him. I heard things like, "We got rid of the scum. This was an honest, virtuous shooting. We got a bad kid off the streets." In my mind, this was an oversimplified narrative of a complex human life. Just because Zachary was a truant doing bad things didn't mean he deserved to die. He was just a young kid making a ton of stupid mistakes. He deserved a second chance in life—everybody does. I don't believe a person's book of life is written when they make mistakes in their teens. There is so much time left for redemption. I'm living proof of this.

My father's message about everyone being entitled to recover from their mistakes kept ringing in my head. I kept thinking about all the second chances I'd been given in my life. I was a bit like Zachary when I was a kid—no drugs, but I made so many dumb mistakes and got into so much trouble at school and in life. I shared my story with the press. "The man standing before you today should never have been a lawyer. I was on a bad path and would have probably ended up in jail. I certainly wasn't thinking about law school or any school at all when I was a teen-ager. But I was given a bunch of chances by a bunch of people who cared and who were not willing to write me off. Enough people talked me off the ledge and kept me on the straight and narrow to see me through my terrible teen years. I easily could have been derailed. So, man, let's not just write off this nineteen-year-old kid! Who knows what he might have contributed to the world later in his life? We're a country of second chances. Look at what a second chance gave me."

I pleaded with the press to stop using the boy's mistakes as an excuse not to focus on the important aspects of the case—the illegality of the shooting. "Are we really going to close the book on this kid? Do we really think it's okay that Zachary never got a second, third, and fourth quarter in the game of life? Are we going to take every nineteen-year-old who's not on a clear path and automatically relegate them to dying or the junk heap? Really? We're not going to even give them a shot at a comeback?" The message resonated and helped shift the narrative around the case. With every new development in the case, Ronnie and I would hold a press conference. Our constant presence in the media and consistent messaging started to sway hearts and minds. Public sympathy for the Hammond family was ignited.

As the facts became clearer, pressure grew for the town of Seneca to come clean about the tragic murder of Zachary

Hammond and the terrible mishandling of the case, including Officer Tiller's police record. In March 2016, the town settled the case with the Hammond family for $2.15 million—even though they had been told in court that there was a million-dollar cap because Seneca only had a million dollars of liability insurance. The pressure on the town had become so heavy that the additional money was found.

Somewhere in the middle of this tragic and now very public case, Zachary's mom, Angie, who was a shy woman when I first met her, found her voice. She wanted to protect other people's kids by changing the law, and she used some of the settlement money to bring about important changes. Today, most South Carolina law enforcement agencies prohibit officers from shooting anyone in a moving car unless someone's life is in danger. It's an important rule because if you kill or injure a driver, the car becomes an uncontrolled missile, even at only thirty or forty miles an hour. This means other people in the car might be wounded. In the case of Zachary, the shots could have killed Tori Morton in the passenger seat. In other cases, children and other innocent victims could be shot. Thanks to Angie's courage and perseverance, this new rule was adopted by many police departments in South Carolina.

The Zachary Hammond shooting was the first time Ronnie and I worked on a case that rose to the national spotlight. It taught us how to shape the narrative and work with the press. We learned the power of exposing wrongdoing outside the courtroom and using media attention to put pressure on people and institutions when they don't tell the truth. This forces light and transparency on important health and safety issues and helps compel the courts to do the right thing. Like my father's lesson to not judge people for their mistakes, the lessons I learned from the Zachary Hammond case would stay with me and continue to shape the trajectory of my legal career.

CHAPTER 12

THE UNIVERSE DEFINITELY HAS A SENSE OF HUMOR

*"It is not in the stars to hold our destiny
but in ourselves."*

—*William Shakespeare*

T here are moments in life when you know everything that came before was simply a stepping stone toward something larger. A seemingly ordinary thing happens—the phone rings, someone knocks on the door, an opportunity presents itself—but immediately, you sense that it's extraordinary. It's the moment you've been preparing for your whole life. Just one minute earlier, you'd been going about your business. Just one minute earlier, you didn't understand when, if ever, all your commitment, all your discipline, all your hard work, all your blood, sweat, and tears would come into play. Until that extraordinary moment, the *when* wasn't really your focus—the work was. But then this moment happens, and suddenly *everything* makes sense. You understand completely that it's time to summon all you've learned, every skill you've honed, and every principle you've held dear, because going forward, they will all come into play and help you achieve something monumental.

My recollection is that it was September 10, 2021, when my colleague, attorney Mark Tinsley, called to ask me if I wanted to talk with a victim of Hampton County attorney Alex Murdaugh. While I didn't know the full extent of Murdaugh's crimes at the time—and couldn't quite believe some of the claims and odd behavior I was hearing about on the call—I knew instantly that Ronnie and I were supposed to play a role and dig into this case with all our discipline, professional skills, and passion for justice. This was our moment.

As Mark spoke on the phone, I listened and kept an open mind about Murdaugh, just as my father had taught me to do with everyone. But things just didn't make sense. The growing list of strange incidents, missing money, injuries, and dead bodies was beginning to reveal a disturbing pattern riddled with alleged crimes.

February 26, 2018—Alex Murdaugh's longtime housekeeper Gloria Satterfield dies from injuries sustained from a February 2 fall down the front stairs of the Murdaugh's home in Moselle, South Carolina.

April 18, 2019—Alex Murdaugh's son Paul is charged with three counts in connection with a deadly boat crash in February of that year. Witnesses reported that Paul had drunkenly crashed the Murdaugh family boat into a bridge, throwing several passengers into the water and killing nineteen-year-old Mallory Beach.

June 7, 2021—Alex Murdaugh calls 911 to report that his wife, Maggie, and son Paul have been shot.

June 22, 2021—State officials announce the reopening of an investigation into the death of a teenager named Stephen Smith who had been the victim of what had been called a hit-and-run on a road near the Murdaugh property in 2015.

September 4, 2021—Murdaugh calls 911 from the side of a road not far from his home and says he's been shot in the head. He claims the shooter pulled up beside him while he was inspecting a flat tire.

September 6, 2021—Murdaugh releases a statement saying that he has resigned from his family's law firm to enter drug rehabilitation and that he has "made a lot of decisions that I truly regret." Hours later, the law firm Peters, Murdaugh, Parker, Eltzroth & Detrick releases a statement alleging that Murdaugh had misappropriated millions in law firm and client funds.

September 8, 2021—The South Carolina Supreme Court indefinitely suspends Murdaugh's license to practice law.

Everything looked increasingly strange and suspicious. We all felt there was something ominous lurking just below the surface—and when we started digging, we could not believe what we found. For those of you who didn't join the millions of people around the world who followed the Murdaugh trial, here's a little primer to bring you up to speed—and, spoiler alert, he's now in prison for the rest of his life for a double murder conviction and pleading guilty to a multitude of financial crimes on both the state and federal level.

As I saw it, Alex Murdaugh manipulated, deceived, and terrorized the South Carolina Lowcountry, specifically Hampton County, for decades before finally being brought to justice. He was the supreme beneficiary of a powerful family legal dynasty, well-established law firm, and political good ol' boys network that frequently played by its own set of rules. From what I'd learned, it appeared that some members of the Murdaugh family, the law firm, and their confidants were not simply participants in the Hampton County establishment; they *were* the establishment. In fact, prior to his fall from grace, Alex Murdaugh was arguably the most powerful man in the county, which is about eighty miles west of Charleston and has a population of about eighteen thousand— and that power dates back hundreds of years. Alex Murdaugh's lineage stems from Lazarus Brown Murdaugh. Born in the British Colony of Virginia in 1774, Lazarus Brown Murdaugh moved to South Carolina in the early 1800s and quickly turned Hampton County into what many locals called "Murdaugh Country." From where I sat, the family's attorneys seemed to hold sway over the 14th Circuit Solicitor's Office for the better part of one hundred years, with four generations of Murdaughs serving as either chief or assistant solicitors.

This affluent and influential family wielded enormous judicial and political power in the area. People respected and deferred to the Murdaugh family. It was well understood that they were not people to be trifled with or challenged. In taking on this case, Ronnie and I would once again be ruffling establishment feathers and asking people to dramatically change their perceptions of a man and a family they'd known and respected their whole lives. Alex Murdaugh's friendly personality had helped him develop strong relationships with a lot of people across the social, economic, and educational spectrum of Hampton County and in Columbia political circles.

He was on good terms with law enforcement officials, politicians, judges, powerful lawyers, and local business owners. He was charismatic, and people liked him and looked up to him. As lead prosecutor Creighton Waters told *People* magazine, Murdaugh's "main weapon was trust."

In the beginning, perceptions of a benevolent Alex Murdaugh were a daunting hurdle for Ronnie and me to overcome. But make no mistake, we were not going to be kowtowed. We'd been in this scenario before—maybe not at the same scale, but we knew the drill. We just had to stay the course and things would start to unravel for Murdaugh. We were uncovering too many damning, ruinous facts for people to ignore. Within a couple of days of Mark's phone call, a truly shocking picture had begun to emerge. Our law firm filed its first civil suit against Murdaugh, Cory Fleming, Chad Westendorf, the law firm of Moss, Kuhn & Fleming, and Palmetto State Bank on September 15, 2021, alleging they had either stolen or assisted in the stealing of millions from Gloria Satterfield, who had been the Murdaugh family's housekeeper and had died as the result of injuries sustained in a fall outside their home on February 2, 2018. Gloria had worked for the family for two decades and was so much more than the "housekeeper" she was portrayed to be in the press. She had helped raise Alex and Maggie Murdaugh's sons, Buster and Paul, and had worked for all of the Murdaugh siblings at different times, as well as Alex's parents. Gloria left behind two young adult sons, Brian and Michael ("Tony"), who were not only left motherless after her death but also close to penniless.

As soon as the facts became clear, I started working with the national press to break the protective bubble around Alex Murdaugh and reshape the narrative. Here's a fall 2021 interview I did with CNN news anchor Erin Burnett:

Erin Burnett: So, Eric, what was the family's reaction today when they learned that Murdaugh was charged?

Me: Well, it was surreal, Erin, they're shocked. You know in three weeks they learned that $4.3 million was stolen from them. They learned that a criminal investigation is opening up regarding their mother's death, and today they learned that somebody that they had great respect for, revered, and thought was a family member, is now criminally charged with stealing their money. It's like we're in the middle of a three-ring circus. Every day is a new level of, well, disgust, quite frankly, regarding Alex Murdaugh.

Erin Burnett: So, let me ask you—because I know you mentioned the $4.3 million that you say Murdaugh stole from Ms. Satterfield's estate—you're saying that this family was not even aware that all these settlements were filed, right? They didn't even know about this amount? Then, they find out about the amount and . . . do you have any idea what he did with that money?

Me: We know it went to an account at Bank of America, and we know that in that same bank account, a lot of the money that he is alleged to have stolen from his law firm went into the bank account. It's kind of hard, I guess, to get rid of $3.6 million, which is the total amount which he got from my clients'—and then, supposedly, $10 million from his law firm. It will be interesting to see. We have a subpoena out to the Bank of America, and we expect that subpoena is going to be complied with within the next day or two. It should tell us where that money went. But for his crime, Erin, it's not where the money went—he could have given it to Mother Teresa—it was stealing it, which got him criminally charged today.

Once again, my big mouth was proving to be a key professional asset. This time, I was going to use it to help bring down a person who was revealing himself to be one of the most sinister men I'd ever met—and certainly the most devious lawyer Ronnie and I had ever come across in litigation. A short time later, after we filed our suit, authorities announced that the investigation into the death of Gloria Satterfield was being reopened.

That same week, on September 14, 2021, authorities announced that Murdaugh had admitted asking a former client, Curtis Edward Smith, to shoot and kill him on September 4 so that Murdaugh's surviving son, Richard (known as Buster), could collect the insurance. Smith was arrested on charges of assisted suicide, assault and battery of a highly aggravated nature, pointing and presenting a firearm, insurance fraud, and conspiracy to commit insurance fraud. A day later, Murdaugh was arrested and charged with fraud and conspiracy in the September 4 alleged suicide scheme. His lawyers said Murdaugh was depressed due to the loss of his family and was allegedly struggling to stop abusing opioids when he came up with the plan. Murdaugh, they said, would check into a rehab facility in Florida. A judge released him but ordered him to surrender his passport.

As all of this was taking place, Ronnie and I, with our legal associate Scott Mongillo, a former Marine and Citadel graduate, were working diligently behind the scenes to build the Satterfield case. The irony is that the Satterfield theft would never have been discovered—and no case would have been brought against Murdaugh and others—but for the tenacity of a self-professed "pesky" South Carolina journalist named Mandy Matney, who'd sunk her teeth into "everything Murdaugh" two years earlier and discovered one of the two publicly filed documents in the Satterfield case. In a five-month span, Mandy wrote two major articles about the mysterious Gloria Satterfield wrongful death settlement. Fortunately, Gloria's siblings read the articles. Due to Matney's articles and her podcast with cohost Liz Farrell, called *Murdaugh Murders*, the Satterfield matters were front and center in the media for months. The podcast provided a platform for me to educate the public about the depths of the Satterfield betrayal by Murdaugh and others. I owe so much to Mandy and Liz.

By early October, not only was our case against Alex Murdaugh ready, but we were increasingly confident we could recover millions for the Satterfields from a number of sources, including but not limited to banks, law firms, lawyers, and a personal representative. We were also confident we could get a conviction against Murdaugh and his accomplices for these actions. On October 14, 2021, police arrested Alex Murdaugh at a Florida drug detoxification center and charged him. He was jailed in Richland County, South Carolina, with a bond hearing set for October 19, 2021.

I'm not being dramatic when I say that at this point, I realized that helping expose and convict Alex Murdaugh was my destiny. I believe Ronnie and Scott felt the same. Even before I could fully comprehend the role that I would play in the growing number of criminal charges against Murdaugh, I knew my entire career had prepared me for this epic battle— all of the cases against established law firms and lawyers, my outsider's advantage, my big mouth, my tenacity, my strong working relationship with the press, and most importantly, my highly effective legal partnership with Ronnie Richter. They would all play important roles as Murdaugh's criminal trials and troubles progressed.

To convince me even further that this was our destiny, a twist of fate befitting a Greek tragedy pitted me and Ronnie against a former nemesis. Who was Alex Murdaugh's lead defense attorney? Senator Dick Harpootlian! Remember my story that Harpootlian was the man who'd helped me build my law practice and then seemed to try to hurt it when I refused his "request" not to work with Ronnie? Folks, you can't make this stuff up! The stakes in the Murdaugh trials could not have been higher for all of us. But lucky for the Bland Richter law firm and the rest of the prosecution team, Harpootlian appeared to me and others to have made a lot of very public mistakes. When I look back on it all now, I have to laugh at how the trial of Alex Murdaugh would literally flip people's perceptions of me and Harpootlian—his for the worse and mine for the better. Perhaps the universe does have a sense of humor. Actually, I *know* it does. Truth is, it gave me no small amount of pleasure to watch the tides turn as Harpootlian became fortune's fool.

CHAPTER 13

GET COMFORTABLE BEING UNCOMFORTABLE

"He who does not punish evil, commands it to be done."

—*Leonardo da Vinci*

From the moment we filed our first complaint against Alex Murdaugh, Ronnie and I worked in top form to achieve a successful outcome for our first clients, the Satterfield family, and others. There would be many financial and criminal complaints against Murdaugh in the coming months. We would end up representing six victims. But this first case set the tone for a courtroom battle against a powerful and connected man who seemed to me to stop at nothing to get what he wanted. The Murdaugh cases would be the toughest, most complex, and most important of our careers. But we also knew that in his face-off with our legal team and the formidable prosecution team led by attorney Creighton Waters, Alex Murdaugh had finally met his match. Over the course of our careers, Ronnie and I had battled many prominent lawyers from local, regional, and national law firms—and won. I believe we have brought more cases and claims against other lawyers than any other law firm in the state of South Carolina—and we certainly planned to win our cases against Alex Murdaugh.

On the morning of Tuesday, October 16, 2021, the Bland Richter team suited up and headed over to the Richland County Courthouse in the heart of downtown Columbia, South Carolina. Murdaugh's bond hearing was set to begin at 10:00 a.m. before Judge Clifton Newman. The courtroom was so packed that they had to slide back a folding partition to connect a separate courtroom with the main courtroom so everyone could see. The hearing was also televised, with hundreds of journalists and cameras present.

When this mythic man, Alex Murdaugh—still revered as a highly influential, upstanding citizen and lawyer—entered the courtroom in handcuffs and a dark-blue prison jumpsuit, I believe that's when the world's opinion of him began to shift. In that moment, what I saw was Murdaugh's carefully sculpted image began to shatter. I also saw something else when Murdaugh first entered the courtroom. He looked around for family members and friends he expected to be present to support him. I watched him physically slump when it appeared he did not see a friendly face in the crowd besides his legal team. In that moment, I saw a broken man all alone in the world. In fact, at that exact time, Murdaugh's oldest son, Buster, and Murdaugh's brother John Marvin were hundreds of miles away across the country, gambling together at a casino in Las Vegas, where they were caught by a photographer. A cold reality must have set in for Alex Murdaugh that morning—the world that had bowed to him for decades was now turning its back. Hell, if I hadn't found the man's behavior to be so despicable, I might have even felt sorry for him. Instead, I was relieved he was finally behind bars. It was my hope he would stay there forever.

After the state and defense made their arguments for and against bail, it was Bland Richter's turn. Before I got up to speak, I turned around and looked at the many cameras in the back of the courtroom. The gravity of the proceeding hit me hard. I realized that this was my chance to show the world the kind of lawyer I was. But I would be less than honest if I said I wasn't a little bit unnerved by the entire proceeding.

"Today is the day that Alex Murdaugh needs to get comfortable being uncomfortable," I told the court. With this public statement, I was also talking to myself. Murdaugh would have to get comfortable being uncomfortable behind bars, and Ronnie and I would have to get comfortable playing the uncomfortable role of David taking on Goliath in an epic battle of good versus evil—this time on a global stage. The public and professional scrutiny, especially in the beginning, was extremely intense. But we were determined to meet the challenge. I told Judge Newman that it was time for Alex Murdaugh to drink from the same "cup of justice" that everyone else drinks from. I said that stealing with a pen is no different than stealing with a gun. My reference to the "cup of justice" was picked up by a lot of media outlets and would soon become a household phrase when discussing all things Murdaugh.

As the lead attorney for the state in the Murdaugh case, Creighton Waters thoroughly described the prosecution's position and requested a $200,000 bond with heavy stipulations, such as an ankle bracelet, restraining orders from contacting victims, surrendering his passport, limitations on travel, and remaining under house arrest after leaving treatment for alleged opioid addiction. Ronnie and I followed Waters's lead publicly, but neither of us wanted Murdaugh out on bail. It's rare for someone not facing a capital crime offense to be denied bail, but there were extenuating circumstances in this case. For one thing, based on what I and others saw as Murdaugh's increasingly bizarre behavior, there was growing suspicion that he'd played a role in his wife's and son's deaths. We both thought Murdaugh was too dangerous and a flight risk. We were also concerned that he was moving around assets to avoid paying the Satterfields the money he'd stolen from them. He'd also been criminally charged for using a gun while committing a felony during his faked suicide attempt. So, when Judge Newman asked me to clarify my position about the bond amount, I let loose.

"I would love him not to have a bond," I told the judge. "I would love it if this man was locked up and he couldn't harm anybody else. Our position is that he doesn't deserve bond. He forfeited that right. He stole. He's a liar and a cheat."

Ronnie followed up by outlining how Murdaugh had already blatantly disobeyed court orders in the Satterfield case, misappropriating funds despite clear directives from the court about where those funds should go. "I can't think of a more willful, open, brazen violation of a court order . . ." Ronnie told Judge Newman. "We have great concern that whatever conditions you put on this bond, he will likewise brazenly disregard them."

This was the Bland Richter law firm at its best. I came in hot and emotional, getting everyone riled up to right wrongs. Then, Ronnie came in calm and surgical, slicing away at the issue with a thousand cuts. We were emphatic that Murdaugh had caused tremendous damage to our profession. Lawyers have always battled the age-old canard that they make too much money and can't be trusted. Murdaugh's convictions for enormous client thefts over fourteen years served to feed this narrative. We also argued that he'd made our state the subject of national and international ridicule.

When Judge Newman called a recess and went to his chambers to ponder all of the arguments regarding Murdaugh's bond, Ronnie and I didn't think there was much of a chance that the judge would come back and deny bond—even though we felt strongly that it was the right course of action. As I said, it just wasn't the norm outside capital crime cases. When Judge

Newman returned and told the packed courtroom that he *was* denying bond, we were thrilled. Murdaugh's lead attorney Dick Harpootlian launched to his feet, loudly shouting his objection. Ronnie and I, among others, were shocked. He got combative with Judge Newman and stated that he felt the decision was legally wrong. No matter. The one-two punch that Ronnie and I had delivered had worked. The ruling meant that then fifty-three-year-old Alex Murdaugh would spend weeks, if not months, behind bars. Little did we know at the time, but the disgraced attorney would never leave jail again.

"I think it's a good day for justice," I told reporters outside the courthouse that morning. "The arguments that my partner and I made about lawyers who mistreat and steal from their clients—it's a real stain on our profession, and I think that moved the court. We're pleased. We think that Alex is a danger to not only our clients but society. We think it's a good decision and it's just a good day for justice in our country. Justice won!"

Ronnie added, "The Satterfields got some taste of justice today . . . I really feel like the court appreciated the weight and gravity of this situation. It was important to demonstrate that influence and power do not create a second tier of justice in this state. I think that weighed heavily on the decision to withhold bond in this case."

Murdaugh's legal team appealed to the South Carolina Supreme Court, which remanded that there be a second bail hearing in front of Judge Alison Lee, who was the presiding judge over the grand jury that returned the indictment of charges in connection with the Satterfield theft. The state's supreme court held that in accordance with South Carolina law, she should have presided over the original bond hearing, not Judge Newman. Judge Lee's bond hearing was a no-nonsense event. She agreed that a murder defendant should have the opportunity to have reasonable bail—and her idea of reasonable bail was awesome! She granted Murdaugh bail in the amount of $7 million, which she said had to be posted fully in cash. Of course, Murdaugh did not have that amount of money anymore, so he wasn't able to meet Judge Lee's bond requirement. It was another win for justice.

In the course of this first round of financial indictments, Ronnie and I alleged that the Bank of America had played a role in supporting Murdaugh's multiyear, multivictim money laundering scheme. Our civil suit set forth that in September 2015, Murdaugh had created a DBA bank account at Bank of America in the name of "Forge" while using his own personal social security number to open the account and presenting it as a legitimate corporation for structuring insurance settlements. Murdaugh was the owner of and only authorized signer for this fake Forge account. In late November 2021, to keep the press abreast of the latest developments in the Murdaugh legal matters, we issued a press release announcing we were adding Bank of America to our civil action:

> As detailed herein, [it is alleged that] Bank of America . . . aided and abetted Murdaugh's financial crimes and money laundering. By flexing their own rules and ignoring banking customs, BOA helped Murdaugh establish his fake Forge accounts, which Murdaugh funded with stolen money from the Plaintiffs, as well as other victims and/or PMPED clients. Once he was in possession of his ill-gotten gain, Murdaugh engaged in other suspicious banking conduct which BOA should have identified. For example, from one of Murdaugh's fake BOA accounts, he issued 17 cashier's checks to Charles E. Smith (aka Cousin Eddie) totaling $164,748.76. In addition, Murdaugh transferred huge sums of stolen money from his fake Forge accounts to a personal checking account which Murdaugh also established at BOA. From one such

account, Murdaugh separately issued 254 personal checks to Cousin Eddie totaling $1,825,560.95.

By March 2022, only six months after the initial criminal indictment against Murdaugh, Ronnie and I had recovered in excess of $7.5 million for Satterfield's sons. We'd pursued all the settlements from all the parties that had been sued in connection with their mother's death. And that total did not even include the $4.3 million judgment that we would secure from Alex Murdaugh by June 2022. But initially, the $7.5 million was the only amount the settling parties permitted us to disclose to the public. At the time, we were also prohibited from saying who paid what toward the total. Later, we challenged this gag order, which was heard by Special Referee Walter Tollison. We would also challenge Tollison's decision to deny recovered money to the Satterfields and another family, the Plylers, who had become clients in the Murdaugh case. That's when Tollison ordered us to put in the public record the exact amount we had recovered from all sources. As such, on March 6, 2024, for the first time, we told the public that on behalf of the Satterfields, we'd actual secured monetary settlements totaling $9,360,055.59.

Even though all the money in the world wouldn't give Tony and Brian Satterfield their mother back, we wanted her sons to feel that she had not died in vain. Some of the recovered millions funded a foundation we helped the family set up in their mother's honor. Called Gloria's Gift, the foundation benefits underprivileged Hampton County families and provides Christmas gifts to those who cannot afford them. The beneficiaries are good, law-abiding people who work hard but still struggle to make ends meet. Gloria loved Christmas and always lamented that she could not do more for her sons. You see, despite their immense wealth, the Murdaughs only paid Gloria about $11 an hour. Not only did Gloria Satterfield's case help uncover many other financial crimes committed by Alex

Murdaugh, but it also contributed to keeping the disgraced lawyer in jail, where he could not shatter any more lives. We cherished this bittersweet victory for the Satterfield family and hoped there would be more victories for Murdaugh's many other victims.

The list of truly heartbreaking stories that involved significant deceit and thievery by Alex Murdaugh was extensive and growing. As mentioned, we ended up representing six of his many victims. Not only did Murdaugh steal from Gloria Satterfield and her two orphaned sons, but he also stole a $28,500 settlement from Gloria's sister, Sandra Manning. He was and continues to be an equal opportunity thief who preys upon the most vulnerable, seemingly without remorse. He stole more than $100,000 of settlement money from his close childhood friend Jordan Jinks. He stole money from the family of a young quadriplegic named Hakeem Pinckney. He stole money from a state trooper who was injured on the job. He stole money from a man who lost his wife in a car accident, leaving him to raise five children alone. He even stole from a trust fund meant for two young girls, Alania Plyler Spohn and her sister, Hannah Plyler, who'd lost their mother and brother in a car accident that involved the tire popping on their car. Alania was twelve at the time of the incident and Hannah was eight. Their father was said to be an abusive alcoholic, and the girls were not old enough to manage the million-dollar-plus settlement money, so they were introduced to then attorney Alex Murdaugh, who was supposed to set up a trust to take care of the girls' financial needs until Alania turned eighteen and the funds could be released to her as a legal adult. In this case and others, it was alleged that Murdaugh conspired with banker Russell Laffitte, an officer at Palmetto State Bank who served as conservator for many of Murdaugh's clients. Instead of protecting the Plyler sisters' funds, Laffitte made numerous, large, unsecured loans to Murdaugh and himself. And when Alania turned eighteen, Murdaugh and Laffitte stole from another conservatorship to make the Plyler sisters' trust whole. When a light was finally shined on Murdaugh's financial crimes beginning in 2021, Laffitte, too, was brought to justice. He was tried and convicted in November 2022 in federal court and is now serving time in federal prison. There must be a special place in hell for people who take advantage of the young, weak, and vulnerable, as Murdaugh and his cronies did.

On the cover of this book, did you notice that I'm wearing a vulture pin on the lapel of my suit? It might seem like an odd symbol for a lawyer to wear, but as I'm sure you've noticed by now, I'm not your average lawyer. The story of the vulture pin began at Laffitte's criminal trial, which was one of the most unusual I'd ever witnessed. The case against Laffitte was compelling, and his defense attorneys tried everything to deflect blame and make it seem like Laffitte was just another victim of Alex Murdaugh—but he was not. In the end, the jury would find that Russell Laffitte knew exactly what he was doing, and in this moment, the talented prosecution team led by US Assistant District Attorney Emily Limehouse was making this important point crystal clear to them. Ronnie and I weren't representing anyone in this case, but Laffitte had stolen money from a number of our Murdaugh clients—including but not limited to the Plyler sisters—and they had been asked to testify, so we were present to protect them and their interests. I attended the entire trial. Oddly, one of defense attorney Bart Daniel's failed tactics was asking witnesses whether they were concerned that Bland Richter was trolling for cases in the Murdaugh matters. Daniel went so far as to call us "vulture lawyers" twice during the proceedings. It was a really low blow. We were not and do not troll for cases. We've never been ambulance chasers. We were merely the lawyers for the Satterfields and other Murdaugh victims—and we'd served our clients well. So, what did Bart Daniel expect—that these victims would go to lawyers who had no familiarity with the case? Ronnie and I had foundational knowledge that could help all the Murdaugh victims. That's why many of them sought us out for representation.

After initially being offended by Daniel's insult, I started to think about what vultures really do. They clean up messes made by others—like the messes made by Alex Murdaugh and Russell Laffitte. I decided to tweet out attorney Bart Daniel's slight and wear "vulture lawyer" as a badge of honor. The moment my post hit the ether, it caught on like wildfire. After a few days, our podcast listeners and social media followers started talking about the positive attributes of what they decided to call "vulture culture." Ronnie and I even ordered vulture pins, which we both still wear proudly. Soon, our fans also started wearing "vulture culture" merchandise. Once again, we'd turned an insult into a movement. Moments like these serve as reminders that problems and criticism come down to your perspective about them. If life or an adversary throws a lemon at you, turn it into lemonade.

* * *

On July 14, 2022, Alex Murdaugh was indicted on two counts of murder for the deaths of his wife, Maggie, and their son Paul on June 7, 2021. The prosecution, led by the brilliant Assistant Attorney General Creighton Waters, Attorney General Alan Wilson, and former Assistant Solicitor John Meadors, said Murdaugh had fatally shot Maggie with a rifle and Paul with a shotgun. Before the trial even started with jury selection at the end of January 2023, Murdaugh had been indicted by a state grand jury on nine counts of tax evasion. In December, prosecutors said he had defrauded a wide range of people for about $8.8 million—an amount that would later grow to $10.5 million. Going forward, two criminal prosecutions fronts—one at the state level, the other at the federal level— would pursue convictions against Alex Murdaugh. Waters and his team would lead the South Carolina prosecution, while Assistant United States District Attorneys Emily Limehouse and Winston Holliday would lead the prosecution team at the federal level. Though these two fronts would rarely intersect in the courtroom, over the course of the next couple of years, they would ultimately create dual strikes that would bring Murdaugh down and provide prison sentences that would extend long past any expected lifespan.

In the beginning, the murder trial would deliver shocking detail after shocking detail, especially when Murdaugh took the stand and started spewing out admissions. For example, he said he was so addicted to opioids like oxycodone that he was taking more than two thousand milligrams a day in the months before the 2021 shooting of his wife and son.

"There were days where I took more than that," Murdaugh told Waters. Murdaugh admitted during cross-examination that he'd even had a pocket full of pills when he was speaking to members of the South Carolina Law Enforcement Division (SLED) after the murder of his family.

He also admitted that he'd lied for nearly two years about his whereabouts the night of the murders. He had maintained that he had *not* been with Paul and Maggie at the dog kennels on the family's hunting estate in Moselle, South Carolina, where the pair had been found slain. Though he still denied killing his wife and son, he testified, "I lied about being down there, and I'm so sorry that I did."

Of course, this admission came *after* Murdaugh's voice was heard on an audio that had been taken on Paul's phone at the kennels only moments before he and his mother were shot and killed. Murdaugh claimed that he left on a golf cart to go back to the house but said there was no indication of an intruder. As he recounted the events of that fateful evening, I felt my eyebrow cock and looked around the room to see if others were feeling as I did. Did Murdaugh actually expect us to believe this story?

Sensational and disturbing revelations would continue throughout the murder trial, with the evidence of criminal financial behavior admitted into evidence along the way. In the end, the financial indictments would play a key role in encouraging the jury to consider just how widespread Murdaugh's corruption was. It was suggested by the prosecution team that these financial crimes had provided a significant motive for Murdaugh to kill his wife and son in order to divert the attention of lawyers and officials tightening their scrutiny around his finances. The walls had been closing in on Murdaugh for some time. The questions about the missing settlement money for the Satterfield sons was compounded by the reopening of the case around Gloria Satterfield's death in the Murdaugh home. Then, there was Maggie's unwillingness to pledge her interest in the family's Edisto Beach house for a yet another Palmetto State Bank loan that her husband had taken out in May 2021. Additionally, Murdaugh's own law firm had begun questioning him in early June 2021 about the hundreds of thousands of dollars of settlement funds that had gone missing. A June 10, 2021, hearing also loomed regarding Mallory Beach's estate, which was requesting that Murdaugh be held in contempt for his failure to disclose his financial assets. Perhaps none of these events in isolation would have been enough to cause the fatal blow to Murdaugh's deadly charade, but together they were squeezing around him tighter and tighter. Ultimately, pressure breaks pipes.

When Team Murdaugh made the ridiculous pledge to hunt down Maggie and Paul's real killers, it reminded me of the infamous O.J. Simpson trial, when Simpson declared after his not guilty verdict that he would spend the rest of his life searching for the real killers in the murder of his wife, Nicole Brown Simpson, and her good friend Ron Goldman. In the murder trial for Alex Murdaugh, the state of South Carolina knew it had its man. The evidence was overwhelming. There were no phantom killers. Alex Murdaugh had killed his wife and son.

Here's what convinced me that Alex Murdaugh was guilty of these gruesome and unimaginable murders:

1. Since 2016, Murdaugh's annual income had been decreasing. It went from approximately $5 million per year from 2010 to 2015 down to $500,000–$600,000 per year. Even this lesser amount of income would be considered a lot of money by most people, but maybe it was not enough for Murdaugh. Maybe he felt like he needed more money and decided to steal it. Killing Maggie and Paul could have helped to divert attention away from his financial misdeeds. That might seem ridiculous to a normal person, but the more I watched and listened to Murdaugh's testimony, the more I felt he was anything but normal. Maybe to Alex Murdaugh, all this seemed reasonable. In my opinion, everything he said in court painted a picture of a narcissist and psychopath. When his son Paul's boating homicide charges in the death of Mallory Beach unleashed lawyer Mark Tinsley's scrutiny on the Murdaugh family and its finances, I think it jeopardized Alex Murdaugh's many successful financial scams. Maybe Murdaugh thought he was going to be outed as a thief who stole from his clients, partners, and family. As a result, his substantial, ill-gotten income would dry up. That's why I think he needed to deflect the growing scrutiny. My feeling was that in such a narcissistic mind, the killing of his wife and son would make it appear that there was someone attacking his family. Maybe he thought he would make people feel sorry for him and no longer focus on his criminal behavior. How twisted is that?

2. Alex Murdaugh alleged that two people came to his home and murdered Maggie and Paul. But what hit men come to kill two people in a rural area in the Deep

South without bringing their own guns? Everyone knows that if you walk onto a rural property in the dark of the night without an invitation, you could be shot. What executioners come to kill two people with a plan to break into their house, steal two separate guns, and *then* kill their victims? It's simply a preposterous story. Executioners bring their own guns and then dispose of them after the killings.

3. Two killers can't stay completely hidden forever and keep their acts secret without ever telling anyone. One killer often leaves breadcrumbs and give themselves away, similar to the main character in Fyodor Dostoevsky's *Crime and Punishment*. Certainly, the FBI and SLED would have heard chatter or *something* about these killers from their confidential informants. But there was nothing that I was aware of—not a single lead, not a single name.

4. In more than one hundred recorded jail phone calls that were released, Alex Murdaugh never once said, "I am innocent." To my knowledge, he never once asked, "What is being done to find the killers of my wife and son?" or "Do we need to hire our own investigators to find their killers?" Not once.

5. A video at 7:45 p.m. on the night of the killings shows Alex Murdaugh wearing different clothes before and after the killings. Before the killings, he was wearing long khaki pants and a blue button fishing shirt. When law enforcement arrived after the murders, he was wearing a clean white shirt, cargo shorts, and different shoes. Where did the first set of clothes go? Mysteriously, they have yet to be found.

6. For two years, Alex Murdaugh lied to his only living child, Buster, about seeing his mother and brother

two minutes before they were executed. Who does that? In all the testimony, recordings, and interviews I have seen, never once did Alex say, "Oh my God, if I had stayed at the kennels for two just more minutes, I could have prevented their killings."

7. Gunfire in the country is loud and travels a good distance. Alex would have heard it if he had indeed been in the house when Maggie and Paul were shot around 8:54 p.m.

8. When Alex supposedly left the house at 9:04 p.m., he didn't report smelling gunpowder in the air and driving to the kennels to tell Maggie and Paul he was going to see his mother. Alex said he had called Maggie's phone before leaving, but she didn't answer. In reality, both Maggie and Paul were already dead, and their phones showed no activity after 8:51 p.m.

9. The forensic team's phone mapping revealed many inconsistencies with Murdaugh's story about how much time he'd spent at his mother's house. Additionally, the excessive speed with which he drove to and from his mother's house on dark country roads indicated a panicked person trying to cover his tracks and come up with an alibi. Visiting this elderly woman at night who was said to suffer from Alzheimer's or dementia likely provides an easy alibi.

10. Before the murders, Alex Murdaugh had asked his wife, Maggie, to come home from their Edisto Beach house so they could visit his father, Buster, who was dying in a Savannah hospital. In fact, Buster would die three days after Maggie's and Paul's deaths. At the time, Maggie told her sister, "Alex is up to something." But her sister advised Maggie to go home for the hospital

visit, so Maggie did. Yet, Alex never took Maggie to see his father on the night of the murders.

11. When Alex Murdaugh arrived home at around 10:05 p.m. on the night of the murders, he claimed he saw his wife and son lying on the ground, both shot. As a grieving father and husband, I would have collapsed on the ground and embraced them. I would have been covered in their blood and dirt when the police arrived. Instead, Alex Murdaugh's clothes were pristine, with no blood or dirt on his shirt or shorts. He even told the police that he turned Paul over and got his phone out of his pocket. What distraught husband and father behaves like this? There was no sign that he had tried to squeeze the life back into them. There was no sign that he had sobbed or tried to hold his dead family members. If that had been me, it would have taken the Jaws of Life to pry my hands away from the bodies of my wife and son. It was obvious to me and the prosecution that Murdaugh's behavior was not that of a mourning father and husband. Looking at this as a father and husband myself, I saw this as the work of a cold-blooded killer.

12. The first thing Alex Murdaugh told the police was a lie. He said he was at the house the entire time after dinner. Then, he blamed the killings on Paul's boating accident that led to Mallory Beach's death. He said that the killers were seeking retribution for her death. There had been death threats against his son, he claimed. The police hadn't even opened their mouths yet, and Murdaugh was already crafting an intricate story of deception. If his son Paul really had been getting death threats, one would think Alex Murdaugh would have reported this to the police months prior to the killings, but he had not.

13. Alex Murdaugh waited forty-two minutes after discovering Maggie's and Paul's bodies to call his only living child, Buster, who was in Rock Hill, South Carolina, with his girlfriend at the time. One would think if that there were killers on the loose, and Alex believed his entire family was at risk, he would have immediately called Buster and told him not to come home and to call the police and seek protection right away. Why would he tell Buster to come home immediately if there were killers stalking the Murdaugh family? In fact, before calling Buster to tell him that his mother and brother were dead, Alex Murdaugh called his brothers, Paul's friends, and a couple of his law partners. He even did an internet search on his phone and looked at some text messages he'd received. The first call any parent should make after such a tragic event should be to their only surviving family member—in this case, Buster. I and others believe he should have been Alex's first phone call. Buster had a right to know immediately about the tragic death of his mother and only sibling.

14. Alex Murdaugh offered a reward to anyone who could find Maggie and Paul's alleged killers but put a ninety-day expiration on it. Again, who does that? Why put a termination date on the search for your family's killers? It was all too bizarre.

There were many more behaviors and events that pointed to Alex Murdaugh's guilt, but the list above offers a taste of the damning evidence against him. By training and practice, I am more naturally aligned with defendants in criminal cases. But in this case, for me, the evidence of guilt was overwhelming. I was not alone. I believe that even if Murdaugh's financial crimes had not been introduced into evidence during his murder trial, all the other evidence still pointed overwhelmingly to his guilt. Throughout the trial, I felt the prosecution needed a champion to counter the defense minions that were spreading false narratives in the media about Alex Murdaugh's innocence. Their narrative laughingly pointed to the prosecution's lack of evidence, accusations of a faulty police investigation, and charges of an infected crime scene. The defense argued with no evidence that the crime scene was not preserved and that this caused the real killers to be able to escape. The truth of the matter is that *all* crime scenes are vulnerable to such charges. The star expert witness during the trial, Kenneth Kinsey confirmed this well-known fact. I have never met a defense attorney who said that a crime scene was perfectly preserved. But it wasn't the crime scene that would convict Alex Murdaugh. His own lies, consistently suspicious and contradictory statements, and bizarre behaviors would lead to his undoing.

CHAPTER 14

A SHARED CUP
OF JUSTICE

"A man dies when he refuses to stand up for justice.
A man dies when he refuses to take a
stand for that which is true."

—*Martin Luther King Jr.*

A s I mentioned, in the fall of 2021, the media, including
nightly TV shows, started asking me for legal analysis of
the various criminal charges and civil cases confronting Alex
Murdaugh. At the time, I was one of the rare voices aligned
with the prosecution, not the defense. The press was skeptical of the murder evidence and felt Murdaugh's lawyers Dick
Harpootlian and Jim Griffin would outclass the various, less
well-known prosecutors. I was on the inside and having ongoing private conversations with lead prosecutor Creighton
Waters before and during the trial about key pieces of evidence
and arguments to be made. An unlikely friendship developed
between us. Creighton was complimentary of the role that

organically developed for me as a media analyst espousing the strength of the government's case against Murdaugh. From my many interactions with Creighton, I knew he would be quite formidable in the courtroom. He is a titan in our profession.

By early 2022, I'd become a regular on Court TV shows hosted by Vinnie Politan and Julie Grant as well as *NewsNation*, hosted by Chris Cuomo and Ashleigh Banfield. I'd also become a frequent guest on Mandy Matney and Liz Farrell's *Murdaugh Murders* podcast. They were relentless in their pursuit of the facts and justice. I admired their work and respected their tenacity and fearlessness in pursuing Murdaugh and his associates. Ultimately, these two podcasters lit a spark that started a fire, shining a bright light on Hampton County's corruption and complicity in some of the Murdaugh family's worst behavior. Mandy and Liz did something transformative with their podcast, and I was thrilled to be a regular guest. They started calling me the "Jackhammer of Justice" on the show, and the name stuck.

In the beginning of the multiyear Murdaugh saga, Mandy, Liz, and I bonded as our reputations were being torn apart by Murdaugh's defense minions, who wanted to silence the *Murdaugh Murders* podcast as well as any disparaging statements made about the Murdaugh family. The social media badgering was incessant. We were gaslit, called names, ridiculed, bullied, and even threatened. For me, this was nothing new, so I was not deterred by it. But for Mandy and Liz, being in the national spotlight—and being scrutinized by people who were never going to even consider their point of view—was an adjustment, to say the least. The three of us supported one another through the madness. We all shared a passion for justice and anger about what we saw as years of injustice when it came to all the bad behavior by lawyers, judges, police officers, administrators, and elected officials who had turned a blind eye or shielded the Murdaugh family from scrutiny and consequences—or worse yet, aided and abetted them. So many wanted to stay in this powerful and influential family's good graces, no matter what they did. It was a travesty. We were determined to shed light on these dark matters. Sunlight is always the best disinfectant.

Throughout the Murdaugh trial, podcasts and social media became very important information channels and complemented the many traditional local and national news outlets covering the story. I was appearing on every type of media channel to make sure people knew what was happening in the Murdaugh case. This intensity of the media frenzy added a layer of scrutiny that Murdaugh and his protectors hadn't experienced before. They couldn't hide out in Hampton County anymore. The whole country—heck, the whole world—was watching and listening. People were mesmerized. This true crime saga was more riveting than most Hollywood movies. There were twists and turns, and unbelievable claims and admissions at every turn. It made people's heads spin! This continuous scrutiny of all things Murdaugh also encouraged the South Carolina judicial system to run its court proceedings in top form. No one could hide behind a shroud of secrecy anymore or count on the good ol' boys network to protect them. Too many people were watching. Many of the judges on the case were upstanding legal professionals, but for those who were not, the gig was finally up. This is exactly why the press is so important; it weeds out bad players.

My collaborative relationship with the media became a major point of leverage in the trial. Either I, Ronnie, or both of us appeared on some type of news channel multiple times a week—and at the height of the trial, often daily. You'd see one of us on before the trial day commenced and then after the trial day ended. In addition to press conferences, newspaper and radio interviews, podcast appearances, and a robust social media presence, we were on the *Today Show, Good Morning America, 48 Hours,* and *Dateline* and were interviewed extensively for the Netflix series *Murdaugh Murders: A Southern Scandal.* I appeared on an *American Greed* special, *Crime Nation*'s Murdaugh special, and a handful of other documentaries. Our media approach was so effective that Murdaugh's legal team—lawyers Dick Harpootlian and Jim Griffin—moved for a gag order against me as early as November 22, 2021. It was never granted, so I kept using my big mouth to expose any injustice I saw. I also commented on the many mistakes Harpootlian and Murdaugh's defense team were making. Additionally, as we collected a treasure trove of information, documents, and evidence through subpoenas and the discovery process, Ronnie and I shared everything with the prosecutors and the public. Over time, we became credible sources for information about all things Murdaugh, feeding the public's daily thirst for information.

As Americans, we like to think that our balance of power comes from the system of checks and balances created by the three separate but coequal branches of government: the legislative branch (which makes the law), the executive branch (which enforces the law), and the judicial branch (which interprets the law). But what happens if there is corruption or collusion in one or more of these branches—just as there appeared to be in Hampton County? What protects democracy and the balance of power then? More importantly, what protects the unfortunate and vulnerable people who must navigate life in a system in which the balance of power has eroded or dissolved? Many of Murdaugh's victims were not seasoned in the legal system. They'd had their lives shattered through automobile accidents, product failures, or medical mistakes that had left them permanently injured and sometimes mourning the loss of a beloved parent, sibling, or child—as was the case with Gloria Satterfield's boys and the Plyler sisters. From my experiences with many of Murdaugh's victims, these were wonderful people who had become financially devastated due to these types of catastrophic events. Some were unable to work and suffered a loss of income; others had massive medical bills due to the need for multiple surgeries or lifelong medical care needs. They all put their trust and confidence in Alex Murdaugh after he'd convinced them he would fight for them and get them the money they needed to survive their financial challenges. Little did they know that their lawyer would use their cases as a means to enrich himself. He put his own interests before the interests of his clients, which violates the lawyer's oath. This type of behavior absolutely enrages me. The case is always owned by the client, not the lawyer.

*   *   *

I believe in the power of a healthy Fourth Estate—the independent media that we all enjoy, and often take for granted, here in the United States. Though imperfect, and sometimes biased, the media is an outsider that can shine a light on corruption, governmental overreach, and injustice. We must never take its important role in society for granted. When media freedom is curtailed, democracy is threatened, plain and simple. One of the defining characteristics of a dictatorship or autocracy is its lack of a free press. You don't have to agree with every media personality or news outlet here in America, but you should respect the important role the press plays collectively in preserving the health of our democracy. It acts as the conscience of the people.

I was a huge admirer of John Robert Lewis, the American politician and civil rights legend who served in the United States House of Representatives for Georgia's 5th congressional district from 1987 until his death in July 2020. He spent his life standing up against injustice and fighting for the dignity of humanity— and he believed strongly in the power of a free press. Even in death, Lewis called upon all of us to bring our highest selves into our daily lives and shine a light on injustice. Lewis wrote a stirring essay shortly before his death. It appeared in *The New York Times* as an opinion piece on July 30, 2020, about two weeks after his funeral. Titled "Together, You Can Redeem the Soul of Our Nation," his essay spoke of the importance of shaking things up, of stirring up "good trouble," a phrase I clung to throughout the Murdaugh trials. Lewis's life and ideas have always moved and inspired me. Here is an excerpt from his final essay:

> While my time here has now come to an end, I want you to know that in the last days and hours of my life you inspired me. You filled me with hope about the next chapter of the great American story when you used your power to make a difference in our society. Millions of people motivated simply by human compassion laid down the burdens of division. Around the country and the world, you set aside race, class, age, language, and nationality to demand respect for human dignity . . .

> Like so many young people today, I was searching for a way out, or some might say a way in, and then I heard the voice of Dr. Martin Luther King Jr. on an old radio. He was talking about the philosophy and discipline of nonviolence. He said we are all complicit when we tolerate injustice. He said it is not enough to say it will get better by and by. He said each of us has a moral obligation to stand up, speak up and speak out. When you see something that is not right, you must say something. You must do something. Democracy is not a state. It is an act, and each generation must do its part to help build what we called the Beloved Community, a nation and world society at peace with itself.

> Ordinary people with extraordinary vision can redeem the soul of America by getting in what I call good trouble, necessary trouble. Voting and participating in the democratic process are key. The vote is

the most powerful nonviolent change agent you have in a democratic society. You must use it because it is not guaranteed. You can lose it.

You must also study and learn the lessons of history because humanity has been involved in this soul-wrenching, existential struggle for a very long time. People on every continent have stood in your shoes, through decades and centuries before you. The truth does not change, and that is why the answers worked out long ago can help you find solutions to the challenges of our time. Continue to build union between movements stretching across the globe because we must put away our willingness to profit from the exploitation of others.

Alex Murdaugh spent a good portion of his life profiting from his exploitation of the most vulnerable of Hampton County—people like the Satterfield family, Hakeem Pinckney (a nineteen-year-old quadriplegic from whom Murdaugh stole millions), and the Plyler sisters. The best way for me to create "good trouble, necessary trouble" was to work with the media to spotlight his criminal behavior and the network that enabled his criminal behavior. This didn't make me popular, but it was the right thing to do—and the strategy paid off for the victims of Alex Murdaugh and the attorneys who stood by them and gave their cause a voice. Seeing lawyers on TV hammering at the judicial system while offering real-time analysis of a high-profile case was new in South Carolina, and in the beginning, it didn't sit well with a lot of people. But public scrutiny of the courts and fellow lawyers was nothing new for me and Ronnie. We'd been doing it for years, and we weren't going to stop just because the pressure was statewide and national, rather than local.

My respect for Mandy and Liz continued to grow. With every episode of the *Murdaugh Murders*, they were putting together more puzzle pieces. They were going deep, whereas many other media outlets were reporting only on the surface. Because I was a regular on their podcast, and Mandy was getting married and honeymooning in Europe for a few weeks, she asked me to create some bonus episodes with Liz. We called these episodes *Cup of Justice*, and they were meant to fill the broadcasting gap while Mandy was away in October and November in 2022. The name originated from Alex Murdaugh's October 2021 bond hearing, when I'd proclaimed, "Everybody should drink from the same cup of justice." These bonus episodes were supposed to be a temporary experiment where we would take a deep dive into how the legal system worked on a national scale. We invited listeners to gain legal knowledge, insights, and tools to hold public agencies and officials accountable. From the very first episode, we knew we were onto something powerful—and once we got started, we never looked back. The three of us officially launched the standalone *Cup of Justice (COJ)* podcast in January 2023. To our surprise, it debuted as the number one true crime podcast in the country and, as of this writing is still routinely a top-one-hundred podcast. We open each show with the phrase, "Cups up!" and I often wear a *Cup of Justice* pin on the lapel of my suit.

Cup of Justice has given the three of us a platform to take on bullies and expose the dark underbelly of our judicial and political systems. We've never been vindictive or tried to grab headlines; we've simply exposed facts and bad behaviors as we've found them. If we think something is impeding justice, we shine a light on it. Our targets can yell and protest all they want, but we arm ourselves with the truth. We stir up "good trouble, necessary trouble," as Lewis called it, to right wrongs—and there were so many wrongs in the Murdaugh case. During the trials, investigations revealed a growing number of public figures and judges tied to what some journalists were calling the "House of Murdaugh."

One of the public figures I criticized was Judge Carmen Mullen of Beaufort, South Carolina, for her role in approving the two separate wrongful death settlements in the Satterfield matter—the first in December 2018 and the second in May 2019. In fact, I was so concerned with the judge's questionable behavior that I even joined in the filing of a grievance against her, alongside First Circuit Solicitor David Pascoe, to the Office of Disciplinary Council and the Commission on Judicial Conduct. My concern arose while the Murdaugh litigation was in full throttle. Mandy and Liz were publicly questioning some of the judge's behaviors associated with the Mallory Beach case, while I was doing research behind the scenes on another suspicious move in the Gloria Satterfield case. In our grievance, Pascoe and I cited Judge Mullen's action of signing off on a settlement where Gloria's heirs were due to get millions. In our complaint, we asserted, "There is now sworn testimony by banker Chad Westendorf who was appointed in December 2018 as the Personal Representative for Gloria Satterfield's estate establishing that Judge Mullen signed the Satterfield order on May 13, 2019, knowing it would not be filed (in the public record) to prevent the litigants in the Mallory Beach matter from learning about Mr. Murdaugh's insurance coverage and his settlement with the Satterfield estate." These were the first public allegations asserting that Judge Mullen was aware her signed settlement order was not going to be filed in court.

Ronnie and I had decided to take Judge Mullen's deposition to find out what had happened in these settlement hearings because there was no record of them having taken place—no court report, no transcript—in other words, no sunlight. Once the press found out and reported that we had noticed Judge Mullen's deposition, I received word directly and indirectly from some powerful South Carolina politicians, lawyers, and judges that it would be a major career mistake if Bland Richter pushed forward with a request for the judge's deposition. In no uncertain terms, Ronnie and I were pressured to rescind our request. We'd seen these types of chessboard moves many times over the years. Some of the same people supporting our media efforts to shine a light on lawyers and law firms in the Murdaugh case would not support shining such a light on one of their own, a state judge. As a founding partner of Bland Richter, and someone responsible for the livelihood of our employees, I had a tough call to make. After discussing it with Ronnie, we decided to withdraw the deposition notice against Judge Mullen but not withdraw the grievance I'd filed against her with the Judicial Commission.

As part of the multipronged prosecution team, we won both the press war and the important courtroom battles. Of course, it was impossible to reverse the betrayal Murdaugh's victims had endured, and we could not restore their broken lives or bring back their lost loved ones. But, in the end, justice was served, even in the face of Murdaugh's multiple appeals and legal maneuvers after the trials. These victories did not come without some pushback. Since the fall of 2021, I have been the recipient of four separate grievances against my law license to South Carolina's Office of Disciplinary Counsel. As I finish this book, these grievances are still pending. The first one was filed by Murdaugh's lead lawyer Dick Harpootlian, who complained about my public statements on TV and in print. He suggested that my statements to the press violated the pretrial publicity rule. I disagreed. My statements conformed with the pretrial publicity rule, as I was responding to the misinformation Harpootlian was peddling to the media. I was also seeking help from the public through the media for more evidence. The second grievance was filed by those aligned with Parker Convenience Store, which is where Paul Murdaugh purchased beer with his big brother's license on the night that Mallory

Beach was thrown from the Murdaugh's family boat and killed in 2019. The company complained about a statement I'd made in the newspaper suggesting that Parker Convenience Store was considering objecting to the court's approval of the $4.3 million judgment that Murdaugh gave to the Satterfields after five months of negotiation. The third grievance was filed by someone in Beaufort who concealed their identity but kept a long list of my public statements in TV interviews, posts on the social media platform X (formerly known as Twitter), and my comments on the *Cup of Justice* podcast. They felt I had inappropriately criticized Special Referee Walter Tollison for not awarding any of the victim pools money from Murdaugh's assets to the Satterfields or the Plyler sisters. The special referee had decided that we'd recovered enough money from various sources for the Satterfields and the Plylers. I disagreed with the ruling and stated publicly I felt it was not just, fair, or equitable. Again, this is full-contact litigation and a war for public sentiment. I have always said that a lawyer isn't practicing good law unless they are willing to hit a case's powerful players solidly on the chin. That's how we practice law at Bland Richter. A prominent Lowcountry lawyer once said that litigating against Ronnie and me was like fighting hand-to-hand combat every day. I view these grievances against my law license as a badge of honor. They speak to my effectiveness inside and outside the courtroom.

As all the cases progressed and turned into indictments, pleas of guilt, and a trial in 2023, we kept shining a spotlight to keep everyone honest. The sheer volume of indictments was startling. The network of corruption that had enabled Alex Murdaugh to get away with his crimes was equally jaw-dropping. And the shocking revelations just kept coming.

On January 23, 2023, jury selection began for Murdaugh's murder trial at the Colleton County Courthouse in Walterboro, South Carolina. Built in 1820, the courthouse had seen many important moments in history take place in its chambers. But I think it's fair to say that the building had never seen a spectacle quite like Alex Murdaugh's murder trial. Though Ronnie and I were not on the prosecution team for the murder case, we still played an important role. In fact, one of the most powerful witnesses at the murder trial was Gloria Satterfield's son Tony. We'd worked closely with Tony and his brother, Brian, on the insurance and settlement fraud side of the case against Murdaugh, so we knew the family well. He'd already been through so much, so it couldn't have been easy to summon the courage to take the stand with the entire world watching on February 3, 2023— but he did, and I was so proud of him. As he stood up in the courtroom to go to the witness chair to be sworn in to testify, I gave him a big hug. Tony is a genuine and deeply religious young man in his early thirties. He's extremely shy and small in stature, but he has a very big heart. He testified about the number of lies Alex Murdaugh had told him and his family about the insurance claim made after his mother's death. He talked about how he revered Alex Murdaugh and considered him family. He talked about how the betrayal and theft of all the recovered insurance money hurt his family financially and spiritually. He couldn't understand why anyone would want to profit off his mother's tragic death, especially Alex Murdaugh. As Tony told the packed courtroom filled with cameras, his mother had been more than just a loyal employee to the Murdaugh family for decades—she'd cared deeply about the entire family. Despite the nerves he must have felt, Tony was an excellent witness. He was articulate, authentic, confident, and compelling. It was clear from the start that his story, strong character, and humble demeanor resonated with the jury. Several of us in the courtroom could see some of the jurors looking at Alex Murdaugh with what looked like contempt throughout Tony's heartfelt testimony. To me, they seemed to be seething as they learned how Murdaugh had exploited Tony and Brian.

When it came time for Tony to be cross-examined, lead defense attorney Dick Harpootlian seemed to completely misread the room. Instead of approaching Tony with respect, Harpootlian attacked the young man in a heated, toe-to-toe grilling. This infuriated me and appeared to infuriate others in the courtroom. Harpootlian tried to blame the insurance theft on Murdaugh's lawyer pal Cory Fleming and said that Tony and his brother had already been made "whole" because of all the money Ronnie and I had recovered on their behalf. Remember, at that point, the recovered money was from other sources, *not* from Murdaugh—so the audacity of Harpootlian's statement was not well received, from where I sat. I believe that after Tony's testimony, many saw Alex Murdaugh as a manipulative, lying, and corrupt man. To watch young Tony vindicate his mother's death and hold his own while Murdaugh looked on and his powerful defense team unleashed their vitriol was truly a sight to behold.

In addition to Tony, there were many other powerful witnesses at the trial. Unfortunately for Alex Murdaugh, his lead defense attorney also mishandled some of those witnesses, in my opinion. The female SLED officers were extremely impressive in their testimony, but Harpootlian tried to make jokes when cross-examining them. These jokes offended some of the jurors I represented and likely many people following the trial. He asked one of SLED officers, Special Agent Worley, "What makes you so special?" And he mocked another, saying, "You threw the phones in the paper bag like it was a can of pork and beans." Later, Harpootlian pointed a semiautomatic rifle at the prosecution's table and said, "Tempting." In my view, none of these stunts won Harpootlian or his client any points with the jury or the public.

Crime scene expert Dr. Kenny Kinsey was the witness who really stole the show. Both highly credible and very likeable, Dr. Kinsey's small-town style coupled with precise, illuminating forensic analysis made people sit up and listen, including the jurors. Some experts during the trial talked *at* you; Dr. Kenny talked *with* you—and his systematic dismantling of many of the defense's claims was highly effective. For example, the defense had brought in a forensic engineer who said that Paul's killer was between five two and five four, so at six four, Alex Murdaugh was too tall to have committed the murders, at least based on ballistic incident reconstruction. Dr. Kinsey laughed and said the killer could have been as tall as six four and either kneeled or held the gun at their waist.

The technology experts who testified about mapping Murdaugh's phone and analyzing his SUV's computer contributed an important story about Murdaugh's actual movements, locations, and the speed with which he drove to his mother's place. Some of the defense experts, on the other hand, were less than credible, in my opinion. In fact, one of them, who testified about the timing of Maggie's and Paul's deaths, said he'd put his hand under Maggie's armpit to pinpoint her time of death, which he claimed was different than the time stated by the prosecution. A number of people in the courtroom reacted to this testimony with laughter. Did Harpootlian and his team really expect the jury to believe their expert's armpit-warmth test over tried-and-true scientific methods? All too often, the defense team behaved like undisciplined children. They were definitely outclassed and outlawyered by the stellar prosecution team composed of attorneys Creighton Waters, Alan Wilson, and John Meadors. The rebuttal closing argument made by Meadors was a real standout in the trial, reminiscent of the dramatic closing statements made by Matlock on the popular legal TV drama.

March 2, 2023, would be another historic moment at the Colleton County Courthouse. With the world watching, this day would mark the official end of the Murdaugh family dynasty and its reign of terror in South Carolina. After less than three hours of deliberation, the twelve-person jury was brought into the packed courtroom and the verdict was read. The jury had unanimously found Alex Murdaugh guilty of two counts of murder and two counts of possession of a weapon during a violent crime. Murdaugh stood in front of the courtroom, trying to stay composed as he listened to each of the four guilty verdicts being read. Then, each juror was polled and asked to confirm their decision. Murdaugh remained serious and calm as all twelve jurors confirmed their guilty verdicts on all counts. I watched the muscles twitching in Alex Murdaugh's jaw as the reality that he would be spending the rest of his life in prison must have shot through him with each mention of "guilty." Throughout the day, Murdaugh's oldest son, Buster, sat stoically in the middle of the crowd. You couldn't help feeling sorry for him as he lost the last member of his family in what was now a three-year ordeal.

Judge Newman, who had remained publicly impartial and reserved throughout the trial, as was his duty, now spoke freely, as was his right. "The evidence of guilt is overwhelming," he told the jurors after commending them for fulfilling their civic duty in the case and ruling according to the rule of law and the evidence presented to them.

The next morning, at the sentencing, Newman offered Murdaugh—who had once practiced law in the same historic courtroom—a chance to speak before handing down his sentence.

"I'm innocent," Murdaugh said, without expressing much emotion, "and I would never under any circumstances hurt my wife, Maggie, and I would never under any circumstances hurt my son Paw Paw." This was the nickname for Murdaugh's murdered younger son, Paul.

"And it might not have been you," Judge Newman replied calmly. "It might have been the monster you've become when you take fifteen, twenty, thirty, forty, fifty, sixty opioid pills."

The courtroom was completely silent as people in the chamber listened to Judge Newman speak. With live feeds televising the event around the world, you could almost hear the global hush.

"Mr. Murdaugh," Judge Newman began in a somber voice. "I sentence you to the State Department of Corrections on each of the murder indictments. In the murder of your wife, Maggie Murdaugh, I sentence you for term for the rest of your natural life. For the murder of Paul Murdaugh, whom you probably loved so much, I sentence you to prison for murdering him for the rest of your natural life. Those sentences will run consecutively. Under the statute involving position during a violent crime, there is no sentence where a life sentence is imposed on other indictments. That is the sentence of the court, and you are remanded to the State Department of Corrections. And officers may carry forth on the imposition."

Judge Newman also added what would become perhaps the most quoted comment during the sentencing. "And I know you have to see Maggie and Paul during the nighttime when you're attempting to go to sleep. I'm sure they come and visit you, I'm sure . . ."

Alex Murdaugh nodded his head and said quietly, "All day, and every night."

"I'm sure," Newman replied. "And they will continue to do so. And reflect on the last time they looked you in the eyes, as you looked the jury in the eyes."

There was no gasp of surprise from the crowd when Murdaugh's consecutive life sentences were handed down. I felt sure there would have been one if Murdaugh had *not* been convicted and given the stiffest of sentences. Even the correctional officer standing directly behind Murdaugh could be seen nodding, as if in agreement. As Judge Newman said, the evidence of guilt was overwhelming. Still, the Judge's words were stinging, especially from such a soft-spoken and wise man. Judge Newman's demeanor and judicial style was a far cry from those in other high-profile cases. Remember the larger-than-life personas of Judge Lance Ito in the O.J. Simpson trial and the probate judge in the Anna Nicole Smith trial? Judge Newman showed the world that South Carolina could manage a mega trial without letting it become a circus. There were no riots when the verdict was read—or destruction of property or burning of police cars. Those who were pro- and anti-Murdaugh remained civil. The world didn't know it at the time, but Judge Newman had lost his forty-year-old son only three weeks before the trial. Yet, this extraordinary man had continued to preside over the trial with grace and dignity. Amid his grief, Judge Newman could have easily sought to postpone the trial or ask another judge to preside. But he didn't. Imagine Judge Newman's pain and horror as he sentenced Murdaugh for *killing* his son Paul, even as he mourned the tragic loss of his own beloved son Brian DeQuincey Newman, who had been the youngest serving Columbia city councilman until his death by cardiac arrest on January 3, 2023. With Brian's death, the world lost a good man and committed civil servant. The contrast between Murdaugh and Judge Newman could not have been clearer. The worst and the best of humanity were on display in the same courtroom. To his credit, Judge Newman stayed composed and even somewhat compassionate toward Murdaugh.

Rather than stand before Judge Newman and ask for mercy and apologize to all the people he'd hurt, betrayed, and let down, Murdaugh simply glared at Judge Newman as the sentence was handed down. It was the end of the road for the now infamous Alex Murdaugh. He was quietly escorted off to prison. For so many of his victims, this moment of justice had to revive their belief in the American judicial system—a belief that Murdaugh had so tarnished during his reign of terror in Hampton County. Alex Murdaugh had stained the legal profession and the state of South Carolina. But now, finally, our profession had proven definitively that this type of behavior would not be tolerated. We were sending Alex Murdaugh to prison for good.

In crime and courtroom movies, this is typically how things end. There's a dramatic high note, a scene that gives the audience a sense of closure and makes everyone feel that justice has been served. The bad guy goes to prison, and there is a collective sigh of relief. Symbolically, yes, March 3, 2023, was one of those moments in the Alex Murdaugh saga. It marked the official end of the Murdaugh dynasty. The family's name would never mean the same thing in the state of South Carolina, or beyond. But the real-world judicial system doesn't work like the movies. Though everyone on the prosecution team was exhausted and relieved, the fight for justice was not over in the Murdaugh case. One week after the conviction, on March 9, 2023, lead defense Attorney Dick Harpootlian filed an appeal. Though vague, the appeal, among other things, will center around Judge Newman's decision to allow the admission of the one hundred or so financial crimes pending against Murdaugh. Ronnie and I had more work to do. What's the saying? Oh, yeah. "No rest for the weary."

CHAPTER 15

AN EPIC BATTLE

"Perseverance is not a long race;
it is many short races one after the other."

—*Walter Elliot*

T he murder trial of Alex Murdaugh was cited as the number one criminal trial in the world in 2023, overshadowing several other high-profile cases, such as the court battle between actors Amber Heard and Johnny Depp, the case of gender discrimination against Robert De Niro and his former assistant, Gwyneth Paltrow's ski collision case, and a slew of big-stakes Wall Street trials. As far as South Carolina history goes, the Murdaugh trial will go down as one of the most notorious—in dubious company with the double murder trial of Susan Smith in 1994, the 2016 death-row sentence of white supremacist Dylann Roof for the killings at Mother Emanuel Church, the conviction of serial killer Donald "Pee Wee" Gaskins in 1976, and the early 2000s money laundering case against former sports agent and USC assistant football coach William "Tank" Black Jr.

Because of the Murdaugh case's notoriety, perhaps I should not have been surprised when media demands actually increased after the verdict had been handed down—but I was. Clearly, the public was hooked. Some days, I'd appear on three to four separate news shows, starting at 6:00 a.m. in the morning and finishing at 11:00 p.m. at night. Interviews were either done live from my house with a camera crew or on Zoom. Mistakenly, I'd been so confident the media attention would subside that I'd scheduled a long-needed knee replacement surgery a week after the trial concluded. I'd reached my limit of getting periodic cortisone shots and was dealing with bone-on-bone pain. Many years of weight lifting, triathlons, and skiing had destroyed my knees. I scheduled the surgery for March 14, 2023, at MUSC in Charleston, South Carolina. I decided to go with a surgeon who specialized in robotic knee replacement. My device was designed for athletes. I was told the surgery would hurt, but that didn't do justice to the excruciating pain I experienced post-op. Still, I did two television interviews from my hospital bed on the day of the surgery. And here's something very eerie but true: the morning after the surgery, I was asked to take my first post-op therapy walk with a walker. My wife, Renée, and I began to walk slowly down the hall and were stopped in our tracks only a few feet from my hospital room when we saw the nameplate on the door immediately next to mine. It said "Murdaugh." No way, right? It turns out someone with the surname Murdaugh was getting orthopedic surgery at the same time I was. I mean really, what are the odds? It was just another sign that being part of the Murdaugh trial was my destiny.

For the first three days after my surgery, I had a pain pump, which made it possible for me to start physical therapy right away. But when I arrived home two days later, the pain pump no longer contained any medicine, and the pain became unbearable. I've had shoulder surgery, three elbow surgeries, and whole slew of knee surgeries. None was nearly as painful as this knee surgery. I was literally bedridden for two and a half months. Nevertheless, I didn't have time to skip a beat. The *Cup of Justice* podcast had to continue weekly. The daily TV appearances and newspaper interviews didn't stop. And filming bits for the many Murdaugh documentaries continued. Also, in the latter part of March 2023, Bland Richter was retained by Sandy Smith, who'd lost her son, Stephen, under mysterious circumstances near the Murdaugh family's property in July 2015. She wanted us to get permission from the state of South Carolina to have her son's body exhumed so a second autopsy could be done. She'd been told her son was killed in a hit-and-run accident but had always questioned that story. She hoped the autopsy would shed light on Stephen's true cause of death. After being retained in the Smith matter, television appearances multiplied. All of this was going on while I was bedridden. To coordinate the autopsy of Stephen's body, I worked closely with Chief Mark Keel of SLED. We developed a strong working relationship as we collaborated to exhume Stephen's body, transfer it to Florida under the protection of a state transport, have the autopsy performed, and return the body to its South Carolina resting place—all without the press or public knowing. So, throughout the spring and summer of 2023, I was still quietly pursuing justice in the Murdaugh case. As I said, there was still work to be done.

Even though Alex Murdaugh's back-to-back life prison sentences without the possibility of parole would most likely ensure he'd never leave prison, all of us on the prosecution side still wanted to make sure his sentences were belt and suspendered. Seeing Murdaugh free outside prison walls over the ensuing years, no matter how unlikely, was not a scenario any of us could stomach. This certainly wasn't going to happen on our watch. Personally, I had seen *way* too much to ever imagine this monster loose in the world again. The only way to ensure Murdaugh would stay in jail for the rest of his life was to secure convictions for his financial crimes *on top* of the two murder convictions. This way, if, God forbid, the murder charges were overturned, the financial crimes would keep Murdaugh behind bars. This was one of many reasons Ronnie and I were driven to keep the financial crimes in the spotlight and on the judicial docket, even after the maximum, consecutive double murder sentences had been handed down by Judge Newman. There was much more at stake for all of Murdaugh's many victims than just money—justice itself was on trial. Ronnie and I were on a mission to make sure that all our clients would be made whole as much as possible. Though we'd already secured significant settlement money for the Satterfield family and other clients, there was more to do on this front.

Immediately after sentencing, Murdaugh had been moved into protective custody at a maximum-security prison in an undisclosed location that separated him from the general population for safety reasons. He lived in a single, eight-by-ten cell with a bed, toilet, and sink. The man who had once enjoyed a life of social status as well as extreme wealth and privilege was now confined to a solitary life with no creature comforts and very limited social contact. If that's not karma, I'm not sure what is. But just because Murdaugh was living in confined quarters didn't mean he was sitting idle. Despite all the evidence and all the indictments, Murdaugh continued his battle to walk free. So began a long phase of judicial appeals and other legal maneuverings. Even in this phase, new revelations about Murdaugh's lies and treachery continued to emerge. As lawyers on the prosecution team, we needed to keep outthinking and outmaneuvering him and his lawyers.

On May 1, 2023, Murdaugh's legal team revealed for the first time that their client had "invented the critical facts" surrounding Gloria Satterfield's initial "trip and fall accident" in 2018 in order to receive millions of dollars in settlement money. A man who is a habitual liar all the sudden got a pang of integrity and decided he would be truthful? Yeah, right. Alex would lie and change his story depending on the audience and the circumstances. Nautilus Insurance, the company that had covered that settlement, immediately filed a civil suit against Alex Murdaugh and others, alleging that it had been defrauded.

"No dogs were involved in the fall of Gloria Satterfield on February 2, 2018," lead defense lawyer Dick Harpootlian and company said in their legal filing. Alex Murdaugh had simply "invented Ms. Satterfield's purported statement that dogs caused her to fall to force his insurers to make a settlement payment." Does it get any more damning than to have a legal team make such statements on behalf of their client? I don't think so.

Only twenty-three days later, the Justice Department announced a twenty-two-count federal indictment against Murdaugh on financial fraud and money laundering charges. Ronnie and I had played a big role in laying the foundation for these charges, as they included allegations that Murdaugh had defrauded the Satterfield's estate and homeowner's insurance carriers by directing settlement claims to his fake "Forge" account at the Bank of America "for his own personal enrichment." Then, On July 16, 2023, lawyers reached a $15 million settlement ahead of a wrongful death trial surrounding the death of nineteen-year-old Mallory Beach in the 2019 boating accident that involved Alex Murdaugh's murdered son, Paul.

On August 15, 2023, there was another legal win to which Ronnie and I had contributed. US District Judge Richard Gergel sentenced Murdaugh's law colleague Cory Fleming to forty months in prison and three years of supervised release after he'd pled guilty to being one of Murdaugh's coconspirators to commit fraud in connection with the Satterfield theft. After completing his initial prison sentence, Fleming must serve an additional nine years in state prison in connection with the sentence later imposed by State Court Judge Newman.

In any criminal case, both the victims and their attorneys have the right to be heard at sentencing hearings. I had previously argued on behalf of the Satterfields at Fleming's federal court sentencings. I was forceful in arguing for serious prison time for

Fleming. I reminded Judge Newman about how he worked with Alex Murdaugh to exploit the Satterfields and steal their money. Like Murdaugh, Fleming was a lawyer gone bad, and I was outraged over the stain he'd left on the legal profession, which is a profession I love. I was not moved by his contrition. It was too little, too late. He was looking for absolution. My response? "You get absolution on Sunday in church, not on a weekday in court." I knew these arguments were only a prelude to those I'd make at Murdaugh's sentencing in both state and federal courts for his pleas of guilt. I couldn't wait to confront Team Murdaugh after three years of doing battle. I would finally have the microphone, and no one could stop me from vindicating my clients and my profession. Fleming still faced a slate of additional charges at the state level, including breach of trust, money laundering, and computer crimes. I responded to his sentencing through a Bland Richter press release:

> I have mixed feelings about Cory Fleming getting sentenced. On the one hand, I am happy that a lawyer, who put himself over the needs of his clients and betrayed their trust is held accountable. On the other hand, I am sad because Cory Fleming's actions stained our profession and caused lasting damage. But in the end, justice was done, and our system worked. Attorneys like Mr. Fleming will continue to pay the price for their criminal acts. Rule of law inevitably will win. You can't outrun it forever.

Dick Harpootlian and his team of Murdaugh defenders would continue to play hardball—or as I called it, grasp at straws. First, they said Judge Newman shouldn't have allowed into evidence the ninety or so financial indictments against Murdaugh, but that was quickly shot down in a posttrial motion for a new trial. By September, Harpootlian's retrial strategy had solidified. On September 5, 2023, he filed a motion seeking a new trial for the murder charges wherein he accused Rebecca Hill, the Colleton County clerk of court, of tampering with the jury during the trial by "advising them not to believe Murdaugh's testimony and other evidence presented by the defense, pressuring them to reach a quick guilty verdict, and even misrepresenting critical and material information to the trial judge in her campaign to remove a juror she believed to be favorable to the defense." Ostensibly, Hill's intention was to sell more copies of her Murdaugh trial book, *Behind the Doors of Justice.*

Again, Harpootlian was reaching. We all knew it was his typical bluster, but it was not in the prosecution's interest to take any of his claims lightly. There was too much at stake to dismiss Harpootlian's ominous words and threats. None of us could fathom a world in which Murdaugh's murder convictions were undone. Hill was facing multiple ethics investigations and possible obstruction of justice. This was serious. This was game on.

Announcing the explosive jury-tampering allegations at a press conference in front of the Court of Appeals on the statehouse grounds, Harpootlian and his team dramatically told the jurors they'd better "lawyer up" because he was coming after them. Murdaugh's lead defense attorney said he would subpoena their text messages, emails, and phone records. He attacked all the jurors, despite the fact that they had willingly given up seven weeks of their lives—away from their families, friends, and work—for nothing more than $15 per day to be jurors in the Murdaugh murder trial. While their identities had been kept from the public for their own safety, they were collectively mocked, dissected, and portrayed in unflattering ways by some in the media. Personally, and professionally, I was offended. These citizens were answering their call to civic duty. Jurors should never be put on trial, and in the Murdaugh case, they'd done nothing wrong. In fact, they'd done everything right and should have been respected for their service. As Winston Churchill once said, in times of peace, the greatest sacrifice a citizen can make is to serve on a jury. Our judicial system, and thus our democracy, only works if we have fair and impartial jurors willing to serve in our civil and criminal trials. I knew Harpootlian's attacks against the Murdaugh jurors would make many citizens less willing to serve on a jury. So, when Ronnie and I heard his comments, the Bland Richter law firm immediately offered free legal representation to any juror who wanted it.

Our goal was to preserve the jurors' anonymity, make sure they were not harassed, and most importantly, preserve their vote of conscience that Murdaugh was indeed guilty. Let me be clear: I would have made the exact same offer if the jury had found Alex Murdaugh *not* guilty. Yes, I wanted Murdaugh to stay in prison. But this was not about protecting the outcome as much as it was about protecting the integrity of the jurors. In the end, we represented five jurors, one of whom was the jury foreperson. After meeting them, I found all to be lovely people who were dedicated and resolute in their verdicts of guilt against Alex Murdaugh. They had listened to seven weeks of testimony from more than seventy witnesses and viewed more than four hundred pieces of evidence. They had used their God-given common sense, their life experiences, and their collective intelligence to follow Judge Newman's instructions and reach a conclusion about Murdaugh's guilt or innocence—and they had *unanimously* decided he was guilty. Each of our juror clients testified that they had not been influenced by anything Colleton County Court Clerk Rebecca Hill may have done or said and said they were offended by Dick Harpootlian's suggestion that they were malleable and could have their consciences so easily manipulated.

In early November 2023, Murdaugh's defense team delivered a really low blow. They filed a bombshell motion over the heads of the local circuit court and asked the South Carolina

Supreme Court for a writ of prohibition against Judge Newman, requesting that he be prevented from presiding over the upcoming November 23 financial trial around the Satterfield's indictments. If accepted, this would prevent Judge Newman from adjudicating Murdaugh's pending motion for a new murder trial as well as prevent him from presiding over any future trials involving Murdaugh. On November 7, I took to X and other social outlets to expose this underhanded legal move:

> Regarding the Writ of Prohibition that Team Murdaugh filed with the South Carolina Supreme Court last week seeking to have Judge Clifton Newman recused from hearing any further Murdaugh matters is classic forum or judge shopping. The traditional and procedurally correct method that should've been used in order to determine whether Judge Newman should be recused required the Murdaugh team first to have actually filed a motion in front of Judge Newman and give him the opportunity to address their allegations against him. The state had rightly filed an opposition to the stay for prohibition by arguing that such an extraordinary writ doesn't lie because the normal remedy of a motion to recuse has not been filed. I agree with the state's response. This is highly disrespectful to this venerable judge. EB

Judge Clifton Newman is the most honorable of judges and represents the best of the legal profession. I'll let some of the press coverage after the murder trial tell this man's extraordinary journey and story. To me, it was no accident that Judge Newman was the official presiding over Murdaugh's trials. Like me, I believe it was his destiny. The day after the consecutive life sentences were handed down to Murdaugh, a *New York Post* article by journalist Dana Kennedy reported the exceptional challenges Judge Newman had overcome to sit in that historic courtroom in Walterboro, South Carolina, and preside over Murdaugh's case. The article, to which I contributed, is titled, "Murdaugh Judge Clifton Newman: From Segregated Schools to 'The Best We Want in our Jurists.'"

> Few watching the six-week trial of convicted double murderer Alex Murdaugh were unmoved by the extraordinary and highly personal 15-minute admonishment that presiding Judge Clifton B. Newman gave the once prominent lawyer before sentencing him to life in prison Friday.
>
> For many South Carolina residents, the optics of watching Newman, 71, who is African American and grew up going to the state's segregated schools, rule with such finality over the fate of the scion of one of the most powerful legal families in the state was astonishing.
>
> So were the sometimes scathing but also heartfelt words Newman spoke to Murdaugh, often sounding more like a pastor than a judge.
>
> "Judge Newman took me to church!" said one long-time observer of the trial who lives in Charleston . . .
>
> Newman grew up in rural Williamsburg County, about 80 miles northwest of Charleston and was the first person in his family born in a hospital, the *Post and Courier* reported.

He left for college at Cleveland State University in Ohio in 1969, having never attended school with a white person in his life. He later went to law school, moved his family back to South Carolina and ultimately became a judge who knew Alex Murdaugh and his family as lawyers.

The Colleton County courthouse in Walterboro, SC, where the Murdaugh trial took place is fronted by a huge Confederate memorial out front. It was also once one of the bases for the notorious, pro-slavery "Fire-eaters" like Robert Barnwell Rhett, a one-time US Senator from the state who gave thundering speeches in the 1830s, '40s and '50s in favor of secession and slaveholder rights — and were credited in part for spurring on what became the Civil War . . .

"Judge Newman represents the best that we want in our jurists," Eric Bland, a prominent Columbia SC attorney who represents the sons of Murdaugh's dead housekeeper, Gloria Satterfield, as well as other Murdaugh victims, told *The Post* Saturday. "He has a reserved, even temperament and has a quiet, heroic commanding presence."

The Murdaugh defense team, led by Harpootlian, was trying to tarnish the reputation of this highly intelligent, humble, venerable, and most dedicated of civil servants along with the judge's most distinguished of careers, which had spanned decades and demonstrated the pursuit of justice in the Palmetto State in several landmark cases. Judge Newman's daughter, Jocelyn, is also a current state court circuit judge in South Carolina. The *New York Post* article above referenced a background piece on Judge Newman by journalist Jennifer Berry

Hawes of the Charleston-based *Post and Courier* newspaper, which provided excellent reporting throughout the Murdaugh trials. Titled, "Murdaugh Cases Overseen by SC Judge Clifton Newman, Who Rose from Segregated Schools to Bench," was posted on the paper's online site on September 2, 2022, and was often referenced as a source of background information on Judge Newman during the trial. For those who want to learn more about this amazing man's accomplishments, and the history he has witnessed in his lifetime, read Hawes's article, and visit the *South Carolina African American History Calendar* online at scafricanamerican.com.

Ultimately, the Honorable Judge Newman would announce his decision to retire at the end of 2023 and seek retired-judge senior status, allowing him to work part-time at his leisure. However, he would recuse himself from Murdaugh's double murder conviction retrial hearings set for early 2024. But Judge Newman would still oversee the financial charges trial set for November 2023 before this major transition. In advance of that trial, Murdaugh decided to plead guilty to many of the ninety-two financial charges against him in the state of South Carolina. In September, he also pled guilty to twenty-three *federal* financial crimes in a federal court. Sentencing was scheduled for April 2024.

CHAPTER 16

THE FIGHT FOR
JUSTICE NEVER ENDS

"Justice will not be served until those who are
unaffected are as outraged as those who are."

—*Benjamin Franklin*

On November 28, 2023, Judge Newman accepted Murdaugh's
guilty plea for all his financial crimes and made his final
judicial comments and decisions in the Murdaugh case before
retiring and recusing himself from the case. He sentenced
Murdaugh to twenty-seven years in state prison for these
crimes, stipulating that the sentences must run consecutively
with the murder sentences and with a promise of no appeal
by the Murdaugh legal team. Murdaugh would have to serve
a total of twenty-three years in state prison with no chance of
early release or parole. Judge Newman's final decision would
ensure that even if Murdaugh's double murder convictions were
overturned on appeal—something none of us could stomach
even considering—the sentence for the financial crimes would

keep him in prison for the rest of his life. Along with restitution for Murdaugh's victims, *this* was a profound victory. With this news, we could all sleep at night again.

The sentencing was also an important day for the victims—or as Ronnie would call them, Murdaugh's "prey." They would finally have their chance to address Murdaugh directly and say their peace. After two years of rigorous investigation by hundreds of lawyers and civil servants to untangle the intricate web of illegal activity Alex Murdaugh had woven, Ronnie and I also wanted to say our piece and set the stage for our clients. I had been waiting so long to look Murdaugh straight in the eyes and tell him what I thought of him. But before I could speak, Harpootlian tried to shut me down and preclude me from saying anything about the defense team or addressing Alex Murdaugh at all. Harpootlian said I was only interested in selling Eric Bland (EB) bobbleheads, which was a merchandise item we'd created to sell and support the Satterfields' new foundation created to honor their mother. Judge Newman ruled against Harpootlian and said that I, as the victims' attorney, had the right to speak. Harpootlian then tried to get Judge Newman to agree that I could only address him. Again, the request was denied. With this backdrop, I opened my court statement facing Judge Newman:

> This day, Your Honor, has been coming for two years. And we're just happy that it's here today. And I just want you to know that we are satisfied that this is a very strong sentence that has been agreed to by the parties. It sends a clarion bell signal to not only attorneys, but to anybody who wants to victimize the vulnerable. This was predatory behavior. This wasn't Enron. It wasn't WorldCom. It wasn't stealing money from faceless people, from shareholders. This was Alex Murdaugh stealing money from those who were closest to him [like] Gloria Satterfield,

who broke bread with him and his family for 22 years—helped raise his kids . . . This is somebody that has tarnished our legal profession and tarnished our state. We've spent the last two years focusing on Mr. Murdaugh; today is when we focus on the victims and the impact that his actions had on victims. I met you, [Judge Newman,] for the first time at the bond hearing of 2021. I had never had the honor of appearing before you before. And during that hearing, I said to you that 'Mr. Murdaugh needs to drink from the same cup of justice that every other criminal defendant has to drink from in our state.' And I think today, he's getting that full cup. It's served hot. And I'm very proud of what our state has done.

Ronnie stepped up to the microphone to address the courtroom next:

What I want you to know about the clients that we represent is that they are the very best of us. That they are humble, that they're God-fearing, that they're honest. That they're hardworking. I've had a great career, but this has been the highlight of my career— to try to restore some faith that was destroyed by that man . . . I want you to know this, too, about the clients that we serve: None of them are victims. And I've heard the word said over and over. I'm even going to disagree with my partner. We don't have a victim in this courtroom. The word connotes that some accident has happened, that some misfortune has befallen them. They are not victims. Prey, your honor, prey is hunted. Prey is hunted by predators. Prey is taken when it's at its most vulnerable. By any way of looking at what happened here, the people we represent are not victims, they are prey. And that man across the courtroom by any measure is a predator. And when I say to you that these people represent the best of us, and I look across the aisle and I see Alex there, who was once a contemporary of ours, all I can think of is for all the power, the privilege, the entitlement that he was born into. For God's sake, all that was ever asked of the man, was you just get up and be Alex Murdaugh every day. To have taken it so afoul is hard to reconcile. He's made his behavior complicated, but we've figured out what he's done. He's tried to hide his true nature from us, but we figured out who he is. So, the only question we're left with is why? And I'll suggest to the court this answer: It doesn't matter because the only person who can answer that question is Alex Murdaugh, and he's demonstrated himself to be quite the cunning liar.

Gloria Satterfield's son Tony followed Ronnie and asked Judge Newman if he could turn and face Murdaugh as he spoke. The judge nodded, and Tony turned and adjusted the microphone at the podium.

"I really don't have words," Tony began. "You lied. You cheated. You stole. You betrayed me and my family and everybody else—and you did so at the expense of my mom's death . . . I want you to know that I forgive you and I will pray for you every day that God gets ahold of your heart." Tony and his family are deeply religious and have an amazing capacity to forgive. They long ago forgave Alex, and I had difficulty grasping it. I would never forgive Alex. I will never forget what he did. I will not give him a pass. But this amazing Christian man had found it in his heart to forgive. Amazing. In my opinion, Alex didn't deserve such grace.

Ginger Hadwin, Gloria's sister, also asked and was granted permission to turn and face Alex Murdaugh directly as she spoke:

> Gloria worked very hard for you for twenty years, for you and your family. She loved Buster and Paul as her own. She loved Maggie, and she trusted and loved you wholeheartedly. She considered you and your family as her own family. To have her loyalty and love betrayed by you is very hard for our family to understand. We just will never understand. And how you were able to profit from her death is especially hard for us to understand and has caused unimaginable hurt to our family . . . If only you had given Tony and Brian just a very small portion of the money you stole from them, they would have appreciated it and been very happy in thinking that you had kept your word, done your legal duty, and looked out for them and their best interest. Instead, you chose to break the law that you had sworn to uphold, be greedy, and look out for your own best interest. Alex, in time, the wrong you did to so many people, may be forgotten. But one hopes that Gloria and her heart, full of kindness and love, will not be forgotten . . . Those children that you stole from— everything—they lost a mother, and you stole every dime from them? I just don't understand. Did you not have a soul?

In all, five citizens and several lawyers representing them spoke to the packed courtroom that day, along with Alex Murdaugh himself. He tried to filibuster, speaking for nearly fifty minutes in what was more of an infomercial than a man showing contrition. At one point, he spoke directly to his son Buster, maintaining his innocence for the murders of Buster's mother and brother. From where I sat, Judge Newman let Murdaugh ramble on, and in so doing, I got to see a true narcissist at work. Murdaugh blamed everyone but himself—podcasters (which was a cut at Mandy, Liz, and me), the media, and all the lawyers, even though his own lawyer Dick Harpootlian made admissions about Murdaugh's guilt, criminal behavior, and drug usage on several national television appearances. The cut against podcasters was especially rich. After Jim Griffin, one of Murdaugh's defense attorneys had spent the last two years relentlessly slamming podcasters on behalf of his client, Griffin himself started a podcast after the trial. Harpootlian himself had never met a microphone he wouldn't grab. Alex Murdaugh blamed everyone and everything for his problems. He actually had the temerity to say that he loved his many victims and hoped they would forgive him.

Perhaps the most powerful victim impact statement that day was delivered by Jordan Jinks, one of Alex Murdaugh's closest childhood friends. He looked at his now disgraced friend with tears in his eyes, wondering how such a longtime confidant could betray him. They had known each other since they were eight years old. Jordan Jinks reminded his boyhood friend and the court of all the times they'd spent together and all the secrets they'd shared. "You wouldn't want me to tell the world what I know about you," he said stoically. He said that maybe there would come a day when he'd visit Murdaugh in prison and remind him about everything. It was chilling. Alex Murdaugh gulped and said he would welcome a prison visit from Jordan, but no one believed him.

November 28, 2023, was a day for Murdaugh's wounded victims to start healing. It was their chance to tell not only Alex Murdaugh and the court but the whole world about the suffering they had endured at the hands of this twisted man. In legalese, these are called "victim impact statements." It's a sterile term for such emotional and personal moments, but that's the law. Our legal system strives to be dispassionate—to follow the rule of law. Sometimes, though, this means the heart of justice must be quieted. Tradition tells us that great judges remain unbiased and impartial even when a case evokes powerful human emotions due to the devastation, pain, and suffering imposed on innocent victims. It's a dichotomy. As a lawyer, I understand and respect the need for impartiality, objectivity, and detachment. But as a man, even in my professional role, it can be a challenging balancing act. My big mouth follows my compassionate heart and sometimes gets me in trouble, but it can also shake things up and give voice to the voiceless. What is in my heart usually ends up inspiring my tongue. Certainly, during the Alex Murdaugh saga, it was hard for all of us to navigate the unnatural tension created by the subdued courtroom proceedings and Murdaugh's barbaric behavior, which continued to ruin lives just outside the courtroom walls. Like many parts of the law, victim impact statements are controversial in legal circles. Some scholars argue that they threaten our Sixth Amendment right to a fair and impartial trial. That's why the statements above were made *after* the Murdaugh financial crimes plea deal had been settled—to ensure they didn't impact the outcome.

Something that *did* influence outcomes throughout the multiyear Murdaugh saga—in the sense that it ensured justice would not be railroaded by power or corruption—was the "good trouble" all of us stirred up to keep a spotlight on the proceedings, including me and my big mouth. The real heroes of this saga are all those who kept daily heat on Team Murdaugh with a never-ending torrent of critical coverage through their podcasts, newspaper articles, press conferences, documentaries, radio programs, and television interviews. This is how the Fourth Estate brought consistent and ongoing pressure to bear on South Carolina's judicial system and prevented Murdaugh's dysfunctional fiefdom from continuing to operate in parts of Hampton County. Though he will stay behind bars for the rest of his life, Murdaugh and his cesspool of bad behavior still need cleaning up. The fight goes on, and will probably go on for years. Ronnie and I will be there as part of the team of dedicated lawyers committed to making sure Murdaugh and his minions drink from the same cup of justice as everyone else—until we drop our mics and are no longer practicing law. Martin Luther King Jr. once said, "Injustice anywhere is a threat to justice everywhere." I believe this with my whole being. Injustice is like a cancer that eats away at otherwise healthy communities and societies. We've uncovered a lot of injustice during the Murdaugh cases, and likely will uncover more. Sadly, the victim impact statements made in Judge Newman's courtroom on November 28, 2023, were not the end of the Murdaugh saga. But for a brief moment, we all took a break and celebrated that we did indeed live in a just society—or at least a society striving to become more just. For a troublemaking kid from the tough side of Philly, it felt good and honorable to be on the right side of this case and help others achieve justice. It felt like I was doing what I had been called to do by a higher power.

In the weeks after the sentencing, letters of gratitude and thoughtful gifts (some homemade) from strangers who appreciated our efforts came pouring into our law offices. To this day, I still get a great kick out of receiving photos from *Cup of Justice* listeners and some of my social media followers who proudly hold up their *Cup of Justice* coffee mugs with a smile of support. This always makes my day. Notwithstanding the foregoing, our job was not done, as we were still representing five of the twelve jurors who had to testify at the retrial hearings. We would play an unofficial role in keeping a spotlight on the case so that Murdaugh could not wriggle out of his convictions and consecutive life sentences.

When the news hit that South Carolina Chief Justice Donald Beatty had assigned Retired Chief Justice Jean Toal of the South Carolina Supreme Court to replace Judge Newman and preside over the motion for a new murder trial for Murdaugh, I was nervous. She and I had a shared history dating back to one of our cases against Nexsen Pruet years earlier. In 2008, she had authored and published a Supreme Court decision against Ronnie and me in *Ex Parte Bland.* Her ruling reversed the decision of Circuit Judge Roger Young, who had listened to two days of testimony, received evidence, and found in our favor and against Nexsen Pruet. In fact, Judge Young called our behavior commendable and consistent with the South Carolina Rules of Professional Conduct regarding a discovery matter. As the first woman to serve as a chief justice on the Supreme Court of South Carolina, Justice Toal was brilliant with regard to the law and held in high esteem by many. I, too, admired her intellect, but I didn't personally like her, a view I'd shared publicly. I felt she played favorites and was extremely territorial when she presided over a courtroom.

I expressed my concerns in no uncertain terms on our *Cup of Justice* podcast and in some tweets on X. Things got heated very quickly. A number of news organizations weighed in and FITSNews covered the controversy an in-depth online article posted on January 8, 2024. Suggestions that I may have violated my professional oath of civility as a lawyer were circulating. Did I go too far? Possibly. There was talk of sanctioning me for some of my comments. But I felt something had to be said. Justice Toal would now decide whether Murdaugh would get a new murder trial based on the jury tampering allegations leveled against Rebecca Hill. The consecutive life sentences that Judge Newman had handed down in March 2023 were now in jeopardy. Make no mistake, the accusations against Hill were substantial, serious, and needed to be investigated. The reason our justice system is the best is because it works for the worst us—even for the Murdaughs of the world—just as it does for the best of us. Alex Murdaugh was entitled to a fair and impartial trial and to be judged by an unbiased jury of his peers. But we all knew what was at stake if Murdaugh was granted a retrial by Justice Toal.

On December 12, 2023, I appeared on the *True Crime Today* podcast with host Tony Brueski to talk about the possibilities of a Murdaugh retrial, the situation with Rebecca Hill, and the numerous other loose threads in the Murdaugh saga. Here are some of the show notes from our discussion:

> As Bland dissects the intricacies of the case, he points to the impact of recent accusations against Becky Hill, who faces allegations of jury tampering. The plot thickens with the arrest of her son, Jeffrey Colton Hill, for wiretapping, further entangling the Murdaugh name in a web of potential criminal activities. These events, as Bland suggests, could play a pivotal role in determining the course of a new trial.
>
> "The investigation in Stephen Smith's death is still very much alive," Bland reassures, despite the temporary diversion of investigative resources due to Murdaugh's other legal battles. He hints at the presence of the Murdaugh name in the case file over 41 times and the ongoing quest for answers in the death of Stephen Smith. Bland shares insights from a recent conversation with Chief Mark Keel, indicating the renewed focus on Smith's case and the hope for breakthroughs from digital evidence yet to be confirmed by SLED. Bland said he has seen no evidence that any Murdaugh was involved in Stephen's death. Bland said that there is one question that Buster Murdaugh was not asked during his lone television interview on the Fox News documentary and that was "whether he has any knowledge or information about how Stephen Smith died."

The conversation takes a turn as Bland addresses the curious dynamics between Sandy Smith's recollection of events and the conflicting accounts provided by the Murdaughs. He expresses optimism for progress, given the active engagement of law enforcement officials, despite the complexities introduced by the wiretapping charges against Hill's son and the ethical inquiries into Becky Hill's conduct.

On January 29, 2024, Justice Jean Toal, after hearing all testimony from both sides of the aisle, announced her decision.

I simply do not believe that the authority of our South Carolina Supreme Court requires a new trial in a very lengthy trial such as this on the strength of some fleeting and foolish comments by a publicity influenced clerk of court. This is a matter within the discretion of a trial judge. And I am the trial judge at this moment. I do not feel that I have abused my discretion when I find that the defendant's motion for a new trial on the factual record before me be denied, and it is so ordered.

Before leaving the bench and adjourning for the day, Justice Toal added, "Now that I've read the record, I say as the successive trial judge that the evidence was overwhelming, and the jury verdict was not surprising." In the end, my fears about Justice Toal were misplaced. She'd handled this complicated judicial situation expertly, as was her duty, and spoken freely afterward, as was her right. Justice Toal openly stated her opinions about Alex Murdaugh. After so many months of fighting for justice, it was gratifying for me to hear this revered justice declare her personal opinions about his guilt in such a forceful manner.

With Justice Toal's announcement, the only recourse left for Alex Murdaugh and his defense team was to go to the Court of Appeals, a move that Harpootlian soon confirmed on CNN when he said, "We go from here to the Court of Appeals—then to South Carolina's Supreme Court, if necessary." Thereafter, if no new trial is granted, Alex Murdaugh could go to federal court on a *habeas corpus* petition and argue that he had received ineffective counsel from his defense attorneys Dick Harpootlian and Jim Griffin.

Throughout this ordeal with Justice Toal, my dad's wisdom kept swirling around in my head. *It's okay to make mistakes. It's what people do when they realize they've made a mistake that matters.* I didn't feel that I'd made a mistake calling out Justice Toal but realized I might have gone too far in the heat of the moment with some of my descriptive language. In addition to what I saw as a fair and just ruling in denying Murdaugh's request for a retrial, Justice Toal had done something else that was extraordinary. We represented the jury foreperson from the Murdaugh murder trial. This woman had previously scheduled and paid for a Bible cruise that was set to embark on Sunday, January 28, for a week. The retrial hearing was scheduled to begin on January 29, 2024, and she was under subpoena to attend. I was asked what could be done to handle this scheduling conflict. I wrote Justice Toal the week before the hearing and explained my client's predicament. I did not expect Justice Toal to offer anything to this witness that would enable her to go on her cruise, but I was willing to go to bat for my client. I even suggested that Justice Toal could leave the hearing open, and this witness could testify on her return from her cruise. To her credit, Justice Toal was understanding and creative. She assembled all of the court personnel, security, press, and various parties and declared that the witness known as Juror Z would testify on Friday, January 26, so she could go on her cruise. It was an amazingly kind act. The Monday morning prior to the start of the retrial hearing, I walked into Justice Toal's chambers and asked if she had a moment to talk. She said, "Of course." It was just the two of us.

"Justice Toal," I said, slowly, "regardless of how you rule, I just want to apologize. I have said some things about you publicly that are no longer accurate. I was wrong. I apologize." I told her I would tell our podcast audience that I was wrong about her. She accepted my apology and we hugged. True to my word, I apologized to her again on the *Cup of Justice* podcast later in the week following the January 30 ruling and on an X post after the retrial hearings:

> Justice was done today by former Chief Justice Jean Toal. She is a decisive and learned judge. I was wrong about how she would preside over this matter and this morning I went to her and told her that regardless of what she decides I was wrong, and that I would say so on my podcast. I felt I owed her an apology. Justice is not always easy and not always pretty. But 11 of those jurors who rendered the verdict were steadfast in their testimony that their verdicts were of their own free will and had no impact by anything that Becky Hill may have said or had done. There is no question that Becky Hill has issues, and they are going to have to be dealt with, but this hearing was about the 12 jurors. Becky Hill was not on trial, nor should she have been. Only time will tell if that day comes. Just another loss for Murdaugh in a long line of losses. EB

Apologizing to Judge Toal was the right thing to do. She deserved my public apology. On January 31, 2024, I received the most extraordinary email from her:

Eric:
I am not much of a podcast follower, but my law clerk encouraged me today to listen to your podcast after our hearing. Thank you for your very kind words. I have never listened to your podcast criticizing me and now I don't have to. You did a very fine job for your juror clients and received some undeserved criticism from defense counsel. Be well. You are a good lawyer, and I was proud to have you in my court.

Best regards,
Jean Toal

I smiled and said a quiet thank-you to my dad for his sage advice. He always told me, "When you are wrong, deal with it in a forthright fashion. Own it."

On April 1, 2024, Federal District Court Judge Richard M. Gergel sentenced Alex Murdaugh in connection with his earlier guilty plea to twenty-four federal financial crimes. The prosecution asked for between twenty-two and twenty-five years of prison time to run concurrently alongside Murdaugh's twenty-seven years of state prison time connected with his 2023 guilty plea of financial crimes in South Carolina. To everyone's surprise, Judge Gergel handed down an *enhanced* sentence of forty years, noting the depravity of Murdaugh's crimes. This meant that even if Murdaugh's murder convictions were reversed in the future, he would still have to serve twenty-three years in state prison and then an additional seventeen years in federal prison. After the sentencing hearing, I gave a statement to the press gathered outside the federal courthouse in Charleston. "This was very personal to Judge Gergel," I told the small crowd. Then, referring to the defense team's tactics, I added, "It was offensive to equate these victims with the Madoff victims, with the Enron victims, or the cryptocurrency of Sam Bankman-Fried's victims, because those are people who wanted to invest money and make money. These victims were not investing money. They lost their loved ones. They lost their son. They lost their mother."

Unfortunately, the fight for justice in the epic saga of Alex Murdaugh and his web of deception and destruction is not over, but therein lies the truth of life itself: nothing of great importance is a destination. It's a never-ending journey of exploration, risk-taking, learning, stumbling, achieving, and growing. Just keep reaching. Keep moving forward. Your grasp reaches but never seems to grab it. That is okay. That is life. Helping to get justice for the victims of Alex Murdaugh was an epic life experience. It was my calling, my destiny to serve on the team that ensured justice was done. But I have much more work to do both inside and outside the courtroom. Sadly, injustice seems to be part of the human condition. But then again, so is the pursuit of justice. And, so, I will fight on for justice with my entire being.

No matter what your calling is, if you choose to do nothing or sit on the sidelines of life, you concede defeat. To live a life of purpose, to make a difference in this world, you have to participate in the hard, daily work—challenges and all. The only promise each day brings is that you can take two steps forward and maybe one step back—as I have throughout my life. But the next day, you've got to get up, dust yourself off, and do it again. You must be grateful that you're still moving forward, and that's what matters. That's how you find your true purpose. Don't get complacent. Each day is a blank canvas for you to paint. No one's going to hand you your destiny. You've got to go find it. Prepare for the moment, and when it arrives, grab it and make it count. In that moment, do what is right and be an agent of change.

I didn't know I was supposed to be a lawyer when I was a kid, but I wasn't really listening to anything but my fears back then. I still face those fears and insecurities every day. They are always there, percolating. But I now see them as superpowers that propel me forward toward my true calling. My fears and insecurities are like rocket fuel, energizing me to be a better person, a stronger person—physically, mentally, emotionally, and spiritually. Being underestimated is simply the best. I love proving others wrong. I know I need to keep improving to make the world more just—even when it's hard and exhausting. Once you recognize your calling in this world, looking back or standing still just isn't a choice anymore.

At its very essence, I believe life on this planet of eight billion or so people compels each of us to seek justice and do good. It's a collective human calling. You might not become a lawyer, but as fellow humans, we all must contribute to a just world. We must give more and take less. We must ensure that no matter our history, our ethnicity, our religion, our education, our social status, our sexual orientation, or our income, we all can drink from the same cup of justice. To make that happen, we must each *become* a cup of justice, bringing our best selves into our daily lives—even in the smallest moments that no one sees. We must *be* just, support righteous causes, and uphold the rule of law. No one is above the law. We must speak up when we witness wrongs. This is how the democracy of a free people is honored and strengthened. The alternative, which is on display in all too many places in the world today, is truly horrifying.

In 1962, the year I was born, American writer and civil rights activist James Baldwin published one of his many powerful essays in *The New York Times*. "Not everything that is faced can be changed," Baldwin wrote, "but nothing can be changed until it is faced." God, does that hit home! I can't change my past—not my childhood, not the bullying, not my fears or mistakes or a multitude of bad decisions. Nor can I undo the terrible things Alex Murdaugh did to so many innocent people—the killings, the deceptions, the stealing. I can't bring back Gloria Satterfield for her sons and family. It's still hard for me to think about all

THE FIGHT FOR JUSTICE NEVER ENDS

the horrible things that happened in Hampton County during Murdaugh's reign of terror—and for so long. It still makes me angry. But all of this is history. It can't be altered.

But there are always plenty of things that can be changed in the here and now, and that's where we must focus our efforts—both in our own lives and in the lives of others. As a young man, I took a look in the mirror and changed my life. I worked hard as a bodybuilder and became stronger so I didn't have to run from the bullies anymore. Throughout our legal careers, Ronnie and I have worked to the best of our abilities to help our clients experience justice. Ronnie, our associate Scott Mongillo, and I helped right Murdaugh's many wrongs against the Satterfields and others. We helped ensure that Alex Murdaugh was put behind bars for life so he couldn't hurt any more people. Yes, there will be appeals and decisions down the road, but for now, Murdaugh will reside where he belongs.

To further the cause of justice, I started the *Cup of Justice* podcast with Mandy and Liz. Our mission is to teach people about our justice system and shed a national spotlight on injustice wherever it may arise. None of this could have happened if I hadn't turned my life around. My life would look very different today if I hadn't started holding myself accountable and doing the necessary work to harness my fears and become a stronger, better person.

Going forward, I will keep facing the hard truths—both my own and those I find in the world around me—because that's the path forward, that's how life gives us opportunities to find purpose and meaning. Progress is made through small, positive, daily steps, habits, and behaviors. This is how we *earn* success and *create* our own luck. A long time ago, I made a promise to myself. I committed to bringing my best self to life's small moments and decisions. I held myself accountable. I began the never-ending journey to discover my true character and life's purpose. So far, it has been a hell of a ride, and I've never looked back. I have lived a good a life and know there are many adventures ahead. However, if I were I to die today, I subscribe to the notion that a life well lived is long enough. I am my father's son, plain and simple. I love my family. I work hard. I live a moral life. Maybe that's something I took for granted before I stared down Alex Murdaugh in a South Carolina courtroom. Though my father is no longer physically by my side, he is always with me in spirit, guiding me with all the powerful life lessons he handed down to his three sons. He still inspires me to continually challenge myself and set big goals—even if there is a chance I may never attain them. But as Ralph Waldo Emerson once famously said, "To find the journey's end in every step of the road, to live the greatest number of good hours, is wisdom." My father ascribed to this philosophy. Don't be deceived by its simplicity; it's the path through which legends are made. Life, with all its twists and turns, is a precious gift. One thing I know for sure is that the journey ahead will continue to be anything but bland.

ACKNOWLEDGMENTS

The convictions that resulted from the multitude of criminal indictments against Alex Murdaugh were only possible because of the herculean dedication of many people working to ensure that justice was done. I would like to acknowledge and thank Mandy Matney, Liz Farrell, David Moses, Beth Braden, Alexandrea Pavlich, Samantha Berlin, John Monk, Anne Emerson, Nick Neville, Teo Clifford, Vinnie Politan, Julie Grant, Ashleigh Banfield, Drew Tripp, Valerie Bauerlein, Michael Dewitt, Craig Melvin, Nancy Grace, Chris Cuomo, and Andrew Miller.

I also want to thank Judge Clifton Newman, Justice Jean Toal, Assistant Attorney General Creighton Waters, and the many SLED agents who worked on the Murdaugh cases, including but not limited to Chief Mark Keel, Agent David Owen, and Agent Tommy Robertson. Additionally, I want to say thank you to attorneys Mark Tinsley and Noah Pines, a good friend and well-regarded criminal lawyer from Atlanta, Georgia, as well as all the other "Jedi Knights of Justice" in the Alex Murdaugh matters, including my good friend Dr. Kenny Kinsey.

Thank you to the Satterfield and Harriott families, the Plyler sisters, Jordan Jinks, Sandy Smith, and the Murdaugh jurors who we represented. They all had the courage to stand up and be heard when it counted.

Additionally, I'd like to thank Kathy Meis, Whitney McDuff, Kaitlin Marcellot, Adam Marcellot, and Natalie Matestic for the tireless hours put in to help me tell my story even when I didn't want to talk about it.

The law firm staff at Bland Richter also deserves a big thank-you. Scott Mongillo has been a great team player, has worked tirelessly for us and our clients, and has added value to all of our cases, as have the firm's paralegal Mary Ellen Shirley and our attorney colleague Chris Moran. A huge thank-you goes to our paralegal Larry Blackmer whose technology-guided document organization, PowerPoint presentations, strategy, and overall intelligence have made me and Ronnie better lawyers. For almost twenty years, they have worked tirelessly behind the scenes to secure justice for our clients. They are not just colleagues; they are my friends.

I want to thank my closest friends, Danny and Cindy Snelgrove, Rob and Lori Lapin, Daniel Hughes, and Chuck and Mary Ellen Thompson, who have all had to put up with my insanity and dogged determination on a daily basis.

I would like to acknowledge my longtime friend Gregorio M. Leon, Jr., who passed away in July 2023. We had some wonderful times together. I want to acknowledge another good friend and colleague who passed away in 2023. He was a lawyer, Citadel graduate and star quarterback, a Lieutenant Colonel and Judge Advocate in the Army National Guard as well as an amazing father and husband. Stanley Myers, we lost you way too soon.

I also want to recognize that this book could not have been possible but for the support and encouragement of *Cup of Justice* listeners and my social media followers. When the going got rough over the last few years, I was able to keep my eye on the ball, hold my head up high, and remain steadfast in the pursuit of justice because I knew that all of you had my back.

Finally, a nod to all the dogs Renée and I have had throughout our marriage. Our "pups of justice" have brought us so much joy over the years.

—EB